ALEXANDER McQUEEN

EVOLUTION

ALEXANDER McQUEEN
EVOLUTION

by Katherine Gleason

Epilogue by Simon Collins
Dean, School of Fashion, Parsons The New School For Design

Race Point
PUBLISHING
www.racepointpub.com
New York, NY

Race Point
PUBLISHING

A division of Book Sales, Inc.
276 Fifth Avenue Suite 206
New York, New York 10001

RACE POINT PUBLISHING and the distinctive Race Point Publishing logo
are trademarks of Book Sales, Inc.

© 2012 by The Book Shop, Ltd.
7 Peter Cooper Road
New York, NY 10010

This 2012 edition published by Race Point Publishing by arrangement with
The Book Shop, Ltd.

EDITOR AND PHOTO RESEARCHER Clare Anthony
DESIGN Tim Palin Creative

ISBN-13: 978-1-937994-00-6

Printed in China

2 4 6 8 10 9 7 5 3 1

www.racepointpub.com

CONTENTS

*Lee Alexander McQueen with his mother,
Joyce, in 2004.*

INTRODUCTION

Lee Alexander McQueen has been called many things, including genius, misogynist, a bull in a china shop, the leading British designer of his generation, angel and devil, *enfant terrible*, elephant *terrible*—a jab at his weight—the Bad Boy of British Fashion, loutish, romantic, provocative, foulmouthed, gifted, rude, influential, the King of Shock, innovative, a brat, a media player, and the Damien Hirst of fashion. He's called himself "a big fat queer" and told journalists he's both shy and modest.

There's a certain amount of myth associated with the man and his rise to fame— uncouth boy from the wrong side of the tracks makes good, attains notoriety and fortune, and hangs out with celebrities. And there are contradictions that make sense in a designer whose work has embodied the contrasts between strength and fragility, tradition and innovation, the fluidity of draped fabric and the severity of his signature sharp tailoring.

The youngest of six children, Lee Alexander was born to Ronald and Joyce McQueen in London on March 17, 1969. The family lived in Stratford in London's East End. His father drove a cab, and his mother stayed home until all the children were out of school. Young Lee exhibited an interest in drawing and women's dresses from an early age. At three, he drew an image of Cinderella "with a tiny waist and a huge gown" on the wall of his sister's bedroom.

The sign outside Anderson & Sheppard, the Savile Row tailor where McQueen became an apprentice at the age of sixteen.

Central Saint Martins School of Art and Design in London.

After the local primary school, Lee attended Rokeby, an all-boys comprehensive school. He was more interested in drawing, bird-watching, and synchronized swimming than in school subjects, and he shared a passion for genealogy with his mother. Although the young McQueen wanted to study art, the story goes that he left school at sixteen and landed a job as an apprentice at Anderson & Sheppard, a traditional Savile Row tailor. While there, McQueen was said to have amused himself by scrawling obscenities in the linings of jackets destined for Prince Charles. However, years later, when these jackets were recalled, there was no evidence of such tampering.

After a few years, McQueen moved to Gieves & Hawkes, another Savile Row house. He learned to cut historical clothing while working for the costume company Bermans & Nathans (later known as Angels), which made the outfits for the original London stage presentation of *Les Misérables*. He then worked for Koji Tatsuno, an avant-garde designer who was backed by Yohji Yamamoto. Intrigued by Romeo Gigli's abilities, McQueen flew to Milan and landed a job as one of Gigli's design assistants.

When McQueen returned to London, he sought a job teaching pattern cutting at Central Saint Martins College of Art and Design. Instead of giving him a paid position, Bobby Hillson, designer, fashion illustrator, and founder of the MA Fashion Course, offered him a spot as a student in her program. McQueen accepted. After sixteen months of hard work, many hours in the studio drawing and redrawing, cutting and sewing and ironing, researching, and the writing of a marketing report, McQueen designed and produced the program's required collection of at least six outfits and was ready to graduate.

Select graduating MA students presented their work at the end of London Fashion week, after the established designers had shown their fall/winter 1992–93 collections. Friends, family, tutors, and fashion industry professionals looking for new talent crowded the British Fashion Council tent at the Duke of York's Headquarters on King's Road in Chelsea. Just as the house lights dimmed and the show was about to start, a small woman rushed in and sat on the stairs. It was Isabella Blow, a stylist who had worked at *Vogue* in New York and at *Tatler* in London before moving to British *Vogue*.

McQueen, long fascinated by history, drew inspiration for his collection from Jack the Ripper, the infamous murderer who preyed on prostitutes on London's East End in the late 1880s. McQueen's interest in this murderer was also personal. Not only did McQueen grow up in the East End, but he had an ancestor who purportedly rented a room to one of the Ripper's victims. The young designer's tailoring skills were evident in his creations, which included a black trouser suit with a jacket that flared at the waist. A pink frock coat, printed with black stripes composed of twigs bearing clusters of thorns, was lined with silk over cuttings of human hair. Worn over a print dress, a black silk jacket with a red lining came to two long points at the front; in back, it stuck out at the waist in a contemporary take on the bustle.

Each signature label sewn into the clothes included a lock of McQueen's own hair caught between layers of transparent acrylic. In Victorian times, locks of hair were often exchanged by lovers, some of whom bought the hair from prostitutes rather than cut their own tresses. In this sense, McQueen's collection served to memorialize the women who died by Jack the Ripper's hand.

Isabella Blow was captivated. She told her husband that McQueen cut fabric "like a god" and that his clothes moved "like birds." Later, she arranged to purchase his entire graduate collection, paying him in cash installments. She generated buzz for her new protégé by wearing McQueen's garments—along with wild hats by milliner Philip Treacy, who would later collaborate with McQueen. When British *Vogue* published a six-page spread about Hilles, Isabella and Detmar Blow's country house, Isabella appeared in McQueen's clothes. She wore the black trouser suit with the flared jacket and the pink frock coat with the thorn pattern from the designer's graduate collection. In the final spread, she and her husband appeared in matching white outfits that McQueen had made especially for them.

Blow not only championed McQueen, but also let him live and work in her London house, as she had Philip Treacy

Jack the Ripper, the East End serial killer who murdered prostitutes in the late 1800s, was never caught or even certainly identified. The story of his killing spree, which dominated the press during the investigation, inspired numerous books and films as well as McQueen's graduate collection.

Two of the garments from McQueen's graduate collection were featured in "Savage Beauty," an exhibition of his work at The Metropolitan Museum of Art in 2011.

Jodie Foster played a twelve-year-old child prostitute in Martin Scorsese's 1976 film Taxi Driver, *which was referenced by McQueen in his fall/winter 1993–94 collection.*

before him. Lee McQueen established his own label under the name Alexander McQueen. According to one story, Blow suggested he use Alexander as it sounded more aristocratic than Lee. In another version of the story, however, McQueen was on the dole, signing on as Lee McQueen, and he didn't want his fashion label to jeopardize his benefits.

The year after McQueen's graduate show, the economy was down, and many fashion designers had given up on London Fashion Week, taking their collections to Paris, Milan, or New York. Only thirteen designers presented catwalk shows in London, compared to forty-six in the late 1980s. Many young designers had great ideas but no money to execute them. To help out, the British Fashion Council sponsored six new talents, including Lee Alexander McQueen. The six designers—McQueen, Abe Hamilton, Copperwheat Blundell, Sonnentag Mulligan, Lisa Johnson, and Paul Frith—were given the opportunity to present their collections at the historic Ritz Hotel, where about sixty designers without catwalk shows were introducing their collections.

The predominant aesthetic of the fall/winter 1993–94 collections was minimalism—except for McQueen's. Sarah Mower, then of *Harper's Bazaar*, described the scene: "It all seemed so hopeless till I was drawn along the corridor by the sound of squawking laughter. It was Isabella Blow, with a Philip Treacy feathered explosion on her head, corralling people towards a rack of razor-sharp tailoring, behind which was a bullet-craniumed cockney boy. It was Alexander McQueen and his first collection."

In this collection, presented in a small hotel room on mismatched hangers on a single clothes rack, McQueen referenced *Taxi Driver*, the 1976 film by Martin Scorsese starring Robert De Niro as a vigilante who rescues a child prostitute. There was a silk coatdress with a quilted and jeweled collar that had cost him two weeks of painstaking work. There were capelets crafted from black feathers, items taken from menswear—frock coats and tailcoats with dramatic silhouettes—and small corseted jackets with intricate Victorian jet beading. Bumsters, a pair of extremely low-cut trousers seemed most connected to the sleazy world of Scorsese's film.

Before long, McQueen's fashion shows, which more and more resembled performance art and shared a sensibility with the

"[McQueen's] clothes move like birds . . . He can cut material like a god."

—Isabella Blow

Isabella Blow and Alexander McQueen. Blow is wearing a jacket from "Dante," McQueen's fall/winter 1996–97 collection.

McQueen splashes down the flooded runway at the end of "La Poupée," his spring/summer 1997 show.

McQueen is applauded after the presentation of his spring/summer 1997 haute couture collection for Givenchy.

fine art of the time, began to generate press. In October 1996, McQueen was appointed chief designer at Givenchy, the legendary French couture house. About a week later, he won the British Designer of the Year award from the British Fashion Council. He won this award three more times—in 1997, 2001, and 2003. In 2003, he also won International Designer of the Year from The Council of Fashion Designers of America, and was awarded a Most Excellent Commander of The British Empire (CBE) by her Majesty the Queen.

In 2000, the Gucci Group bought 51 percent of the Alexander McQueen company, keeping McQueen in place as creative director. A few months later, he left Givenchy and soon expanded his women's- and menswear label into fragrance, eyewear, and accessories. The company also opened flagship stores in New York, Milan, Los Angeles, and Las Vegas. McQueen, among the most acclaimed fashion designers of his time, had become the driving force of an international luxury brand, with a good paycheck, a burgeoning art collection, and prominent friends.

And then McQueen's stellar career came to an abrupt end. On February 2, 2010, Joyce McQueen, the designer's beloved mother, died. Postings on Twitter indicated that he was bereft but determined to go on. On the morning of February 11, however, Lee Alexander McQueen was found in his apartment, dead by his own hand. In a statement made after McQueen's death, Anna Wintour, editor of *Vogue*, called him "one of the greatest talents of his generation," a thought shared by many in fashion and in the world at large.

Alexander McQueen and Philip Treacy come out to greet the audience after McQueen's spring/summer 2008 show, "La Dame Bleue," conceived as a tribute to their friend Isabella Blow, who died in 2007.

> "I try and modify fashion like a scientist by offering what is relevant to today and what will continue to be so tomorrow."
>
> —Alexander McQueen

Alexander McQueen waves to the audience at the end of his spring/summer 2010 show, "Plato's Atlantis."

ALEXANDER McQUEEN
RUNWAY SHOWS

"I need inspiration. I need something to fuel my imagination and the shows are what spur me on, make me excited about what I'm doing."

—Alexander McQueen

NIHILISM

Spring/Summer 1994

Alexander McQueen's first professional catwalk show is presented at the Bluebird Garage on King's Road in Chelsea. Built in 1923 as Europe's largest garage and once a famous local landmark, the formerly glamorous art deco building, which is being used as a clothing market, has gained a bad reputation. Rumor has it that drugs are for sale and there has even been a recent shooting. Although there are no seats, the spectators settle down. The music comes in loud bursts—a hard house beat. Between roars of sound, there is the silence of shock.

Models appear smeared with blood and dirt. Some of them look as if they have just been in a car wreck. Others seem to have suppurating wounds. One covers her bare breasts with bloodstained hands. But what of the clothes? Bumster trousers, pants cut so low that the cleavage of the buttocks is exposed, make another appearance. A white turtleneck dress emphasizes the model's breasts and nipples in much the same way a wet T-shirt does. Has the fabric been laminated or is it see-through at the bust only?

The collection is eclectic, though. In addition to exposed breasts and buttocks and barely there garments, there are also sharp suits and jackets with long, elegant lines. The fabric of a suit in a gray silk and wool blend has a bit of sheen. The thigh-length jacket, worn over extremely low-cut trousers, has turned-back cuffs and an Edwardian feel. A black cotton and silk jacket with a stand-up collar sports lapels that almost meet at the breastbone and then sweep open dashingly on a diagonal. And there's a McQueen T-shirt—marked with the imprint of blood red hands.

A model with her hair pinned up haphazardly wears a pair of black pants lined in red that are slit in the back from the waistband all the way down the leg. Over them, she wears a short sleeveless top that laces along the spine. One of the model's elbows appears to be stained with blood. Another model wears a dress that derives color from an oily grime, tawny at the top and increasingly sheer toward the frayed hem, which hovers at the top of the thigh. A top that looks as though it's been slashed with a knife is worn with thigh-high black tights and a tiny skirt of plastic wrap that isn't quite long enough to conceal that the model isn't wearing anything underneath.

In the *Independent*, in an article titled "McQueen's Theatre of Cruelty," Marion Hume writes: "You could tell there was a consensus: Alexander McQueen's debut was a horror show." And yet she appreciates his traditional skills and adept tailoring, and she even seems to like some of his clothes, stating that McQueen has "something new to say, in a business where designers gorge on each other's ideas." She hopes he will grow out of his "perverse view of women," but notes "he has an assured view of fashion." She concludes, "The shock of the new has to be just that: shocking. If London is to keep its creative supremacy, we must tolerate it."

Opposite page: A model wearing nothing beneath her skirt of plastic wrap covers herself with one hand. When she turns, her buttocks are exposed.

Right, top: Grime seems to ooze from this dress down the model's leg. Her red eye shadow complements her blood-stained hands and ears.

Right, bottom: Not for the timid, McQueen's red-lined, slit-open pants expose the entire back of the model's leg and a good slice of her buttocks.

BANSHEE

Fall/Winter 1994–95

Established designers continue to abandon Fashion Week in London in favor of Paris, Milan, or New York. Many members of the international fashion press and buyers from overseas are following them. Cynics refer to London's three-and-a-half day event as "Fashion Five Minutes." Because manufacturing clothing is still a problem, many designers have turned to an artisanal approach, and are crafting their garments by hand. With his traditional training, years of technical experience, and hot creative vision, twenty-five-year-old Lee Alexander McQueen is becoming a major player.

Isabella Blow has done much to publicize the Alexander McQueen label. She wears the clothes and is adept at getting press. A good number of press people showed for last season's presentation, among them fashion stylist Katie Grand, who, not long after the show, photographed Blow wearing Alexander McQueen for *Dazed & Confused*, the cutting-edge style magazine. This season's show venue is the Café de Paris, a historic nightclub in London's Piccadilly that first opened its doors in 1924.

Editors, buyers, and budding Alexander McQueen fans hustle to their seats. There are a number of young people among the spectators. The atmosphere is expectant. McQueen has named his show after the banshee, a creature from Irish folklore, a female spirit who wails when someone is about to die. The Scottish version of this creature washes the bloodstained clothes and armor of the moribund. Given the blood-soaked images McQueen created last season, this could be a gory show.

*Left: Metallic fabric accentuates the sharply
pointed lapels of this long jacket.*

*Opposite page: This chenille sweaterdress
with a transparent nylon inset is hiked up to
show the detached pant legs in a
wool check worn below.*

Music starts and the models appear in front of stage flats draped in white. One wears a white high-necked dress with an empire waist and a billowing full-length skirt of translucent chiffon. A pregnant skinhead models a sheer black dress with an Elizabethan neckline that exposes her nipples (page 22). On her stubbly head, "McQueen" is spelled out in stenciled silver letters.

A perfectly tailored jacket, hand-printed to resemble the torn layers of a billboard, is paired with a large-collared purple shirt worn over bare legs. And there are more jackets: one in black wool with silver cuffs bears gold military braid; another military style, this time in gray, has a tall stand-up collar and is cropped at the waist. A button-front vest of white resin is worn over hand-painted white cotton trousers. Plaster covers the neck and shoulders of a model in a white chiffon dress. The skirt of a chenille

dress with red sleeves connects to the bodice with invisible threads. On her head, another model in a white dress balances a large gray feather headdress that appears to be an entire squashed bird.

The crowd whoops and cheers. Susannah Barron, writing in the *Guardian*, speculates that McQueen must have many friends in the audience. She concludes that his show "was a festive end to London Fashion Week." Lucinda Alford writes in the *Observer*: "While [McQueen] admits the historical references in his clothing—'Tradition is the basis for everything I do'—he has enough vision to produce clothes that are not historical replicas." Another *Observer* article calls McQueen "star of the week" and continues by explaining that McQueen's presentation demonstrates "an uncompromising view of fashion that triumphantly closed the week."

THE BIRDS

Spring/Summer 1995

Word is McQueen is working with a New York publicist.
Last season, after showing his collection in London,
he traveled to Manhattan and presented his work in a
downtown loft. The collection's presentation got a mention
in The New Yorker—*a profile-raising move. With the help*
of a shop in New York's Greenwich Village called Untitled,
the Alexander McQueen label garnered a six-page spread in
the August 1994 edition of Elle *magazine.*

Some fashion journalists feel that London Fashion Week is coming back, thanks to the new generation of talent, and some cite McQueen as the main draw. This season's show is presented in a ramshackle warehouse called Bagley's, a party space in King's Cross, a rundown neighborhood reputed to be a red-light district. It's dark inside, and the floor is less than clean. The black catwalk is painted like a road with a broken white line down the center.

The collection takes its name from Alfred Hitchcock's 1963 suspense film, in which a small California town is beset by increasingly vicious and aggressive birds. Models in stilettos attached to the feet with cellophane tape emerge from a dark tunnel. They wear white contact lenses and the ends of their hair are frizzed. Underneath frock coats, breasts are bare or covered only with plastic wrap. Tire tracks on clothes and skin make some models look like they've been hit by a car.

A model goes by in a black-and-white jacket, tire tracks on her bare legs and torso (page 26). Plum Sykes, Isabella Blow's intern at British *Vogue*, walks the runway. She wears a trouser suit, the jacket of which is printed with a flock of soaring swallows. She has nothing on under the jacket and holds the lapels closed with one hand. And, of course, there are frock coats and bumster trousers. A backless black coat, shown over black bumsters, is held together with crisscrosses of clear fishing line.

Mr. Pearl, the corset maker, appears in a red swallow-print skirt and a black nipped-in jacket. Spectators gasp at his twenty-inch waist. A white skirt suit bearing tire tracks goes by, then a model who looks as if she is swaddled in plastic wrap. Is that Isabella Blow on the catwalk? Another model's neck and shoulders are encased in layered silver feathers, as if an entire bird has been arrayed around her neck.

In London's *Evening Standard*, Alison Veness reviews London Fashion Week and describes the Alexander McQueen show as the "hot ticket of the weekend." Although Amy M. Spindler of the *New York Times* doesn't like bumster trousers, she writes that Alexander McQueen is "easily the most talked-about designer to be showing this year." She continues by saying that the designer's jackets are "nothing short of perfect." At the end of the show, the mood is euphoric. Surely, with such talent on display, British fashion has a bright future.

"*To me, that part of the body—not so much the buttocks, but the bottom of the spine—that's the most erotic part of anyone's body, man or woman.*"

—Alexander McQueen

Opposite page: *Tire tracks mar the pristine white of this tailored suit jacket.*

Left: *A backless jacket and pair of bumster trousers leave the cleavage of the buttocks exposed.*

HIGHLAND RAPE

Fall/Winter 1995–96

A single sheet of photocopied paper, the show's invitation depicts a five-inch long surgical wound, complete with scabby holes left by the suturing needle. For the first time since his graduate show, Alexander McQueen is showing in the British Fashion Council's official tent. At the show venue outside the Natural History Museum in London's South Kensington there is much excitement. McQueen's is the last presentation of the week. When spectators look at the program, another single photocopied sheet, and see the show's title, some of the excitement turns to jitters. Rape? It's a show about rape?

People love McQueen for being provocative—but now he may have gone too far. To McQueen, however, this show is about the subjugation of the Scots, not the brutalization of women. As he explains: "The Scottish Highlands have been of great inspiration to many designers in the past. But they have been romanticized all too often. There were swathes of tartan but only as protection against the elements. Protection proved not to be enough against the fury of soldiers, as in many places and at many times across the world."

From behind the stage flats, blue and white lights flash, illuminating the top of the catwalk in bursts. The music starts with a crash. A model appears, and a spotlight centers on her. She strides down the catwalk, which is strewn with heather, in a green turtleneck sweater with extra-long sleeves and semi-sheer lace pants that completely cover her shoes, elongating her already lengthy legs. Her long hair is pinned back from her face and hangs loose down the back. Her special effects contact lenses turn her eyes completely black, giving her a spooky, otherworldly power.

A model in a short-sleeved white jacket paired with a stiff green lace skirt wears leather driving gloves that appear to be stained with blood. Is she Lady Macbeth out for a stroll? Another model walks in a tattered lace dress with a gaping hole that reveals her panties and upper thigh. With her cropped hair, mirrored contact lenses, and dark eye makeup, she looks like a fearsome pixie.

When a model in a dress made from cut-out lace flowers reaches the end of the catwalk, she swings her hips and turns, casting a glance over her shoulder. Then she playfully kicks one foot out and moves on. Wearing a green dress slit to expose one breast, a model lurches along the catwalk, her long hair hanging in ropes. Stopping to pose at the end of the catwalk, another model in a gray dress slashed multiple times at the chest actually smiles.

A model in a pair of shiny bumster trousers cut just above the pubic bone clutches the lapels of her laminated lace frock coat. A watch chain dangles from the pubic area of another model in a perfectly tailored tartan skirt. When she poses, she looks down as if just noticing the chain and shoots a quizzical look at the photographers. A model in a breast-baring jacket and McQueen tartan skirt rushes out with a worried air (page 30). There's more McQueen plaid, including trousers that look laminated; an ensemble of tartan, netting, and lace; and a peignoir crafted from wool and black chiffon. A black chiffon dress goes by—worn under a bodice of armor. And a sparkling cropped sweater bears long upright feathers that encircle the model's head.

Writing in the *New York Times*, Amy M. Spindler sums up: "It was a collection packed with restless, rousing ideas, by far the best of the London season." But others disagree. Iain Webb in the *Times* of London writes: "McQueen's radical style has seen him dubbed a rising star (and rightly so), but this latest collection, all torn-lace dresses and ugly sex 'n' violence imagery, sees him fall from favour." Sally Brampton in the *Guardian* is even more severe: "It is McQueen's brand of misogynistic absurdity that gives fashion a bad name."

Above: The upright feathers at the neckline of this sweater create a protective cage for the wearer.

Opposite page: This ensemble mixes the strength of McQueen tartan with the fragility of netting and lace.

THE HUNGER

Spring/Summer 1996

Once again, the Alexander McQueen presentation is the finale of London Fashion Week, and once again, the event is staged in the British Fashion Council's tent outside the Natural History Museum. Attendance by journalists and buyers is said to be up by 30 percent or more. People are eager to see this season's looks, and yet, there's still a sense of frustration, a sense that British designers are not being seen as serious producers of desirable commodities, but rather as a lunatic fringe of experimentation and naughtiness.

McQueen is among the most promising young designers in London, but many find the anger expressed in his collections too off-putting. Others are fed up with his provocative *enfant terrible* antics. But McQueen's ideas are catching on. His decaying lace look and extremely low-cut trousers have been adopted by other designers, a testament to the potential of his vision.

Inspired by the 1983 film *The Hunger*, starring David Bowie and Catherine Deneuve as remarkably sexy vampires, the new Alexander McQueen collection features lots of red, white, black—and strategically bared flesh. McQueen's notorious bumster trousers appear here along with pants that are sliced open at the thigh, skirts that expose one hip, and tops that showcase both the male and the female nipple.

Eyebrows are drawn in long diagonals up the forehead. Many of the models walk with a certain fierceness and aggression. A model in a white skirt and red jacket has a stiff paintbrush of hair rising straight up from her chignon. With no shirt on, she raises her arms, baring her breasts in defiance, and twirls around. Then there's a blue skirt suit, the jacket of which has cutout shoulders. A model in a plaster cast that covers one arm and breast glares at the audience. There are beautiful jackets in gray and a few in more colorful fabrics. Some have revealing cutouts.

A male model in a red shirt gives photographers the finger. Another leans down at the end of the catwalk, mouthing obscenities. An impeccable jacket in gray wool is shown with pants slit open at the rear. A model, dressed in sheer netting with a swath of feathers down the center, flaps her arms and scatters feathers from a plastic bag onto the runway. A shiny silver jacket is worn over a plastic bustier containing live worms (page 34). When McQueen takes his bow to enthusiastic applause, he pulls down his pants and moons the audience.

In the London *Times*, Iain R. Webb writes: "Alexander McQueen certainly generates excitement, and is indeed an extremely clever designer, yet his ideas appear too wrapped up in his angry young man pose." Sally Brampton writing in the *Guardian* says: "If McQueen could only bring himself to curb some of his more childish tantrums and stop savaging that which is potentially beautiful, we might see the stuff of greatness."

Opposite page: In a sheer white dress and a plaster cast complete with graffiti, this model walks with lots of energy and a wary attitude.

Right, top: Feathers frequently appear in McQueen's work. Here, they also get scattered over the runway.

Right, bottom: An embroidered top with kimono-like sleeves is worn over shiny red bumster trousers.

DANTE

Fall/Winter 1996–97

This season's Alexander McQueen show is held in Christ Church Spitalfields in London's East End. It's McQueen's old neighborhood, and the church, which dates back to the 1720s, is where his ancestors were christened. A crowd gathers at the entrance, swarming to get in out of the rain. Moving against the throng, Isabella Blow squirms out of the church to go have a quick drink before the event begins. Inside, calm reigns. Elevated banks of candles surround the columns that support the vaulted ceiling. The runway is shaped like a cross. A human skeleton is seated in the front row.

The show's title references Dante Alighieri, the Italian man of letters, who described heaven and hell in *The Divine Comedy*, which he worked on from 1308 until his death in 1321. McQueen also found inspiration for this collection in fourteenth-century Flemish paintings. War, peace, and peace of mind are also themes. The back of the show's program bears a picture of McQueen as a small child with a puppy. So, innocence, or innocence lost, also comes into play.

On the sound system, choral music is replaced by an insistent beat. The church's stained-glass window glows brightly then goes dark. Male models dressed as gang members swagger out. They place themselves at the ends of the catwalk. Then the women appear, stepping through an archway of roses. Antlers and horns sprout from heads and metal thorns from cheeks. One model wears a silver crown of thorns, while others wear black masks decorated with crucifixes.

Models walk in typically eclectic outfits. An aristocratic beauty takes her turn in a lavender brocade silk corset festooned with jet beading and black lace, paired with a skirt made of frayed denim squares (page 38). It's as if she has left her manor home to run with the London punks. A military jacket is worn over a very short black lace dress. A soft white cashmere dress printed with a black paisley pattern has an unexpected train. And there are close-fitting jackets, some with sleeves that are cut on a spiral and slashed open at the elbow.

In the *Observer*, Karl Plewka and Roger Tredre say, "This time last year, McQueen was one of a number of young emerging designer talents. Now he has moved ahead of the pack and set his own standard." In the *New York Times*, Amy M. Spindler writes that she sees a new maturity in McQueen's work and concludes: "In the past, the lewdness of Mr. McQueen's fantasies has limited the appeal of his inventive designs. This collection could be enjoyed by all."

McQueen is working to expand his appeal and his customer base: he's taking this collection to New York for a second showing. The day before the show, *Women's Wear Daily* runs an interview on the cover. At the venue, a former synagogue on the Lower East Side, there is chaos. A soggy snow falls. Those with invitations and those without jockey to get inside. Anna Wintour, editor of *Vogue*, is among those stuck between parked vans and an iron fence. Finally, one of McQueen's people escorts Wintour and her entourage inside. The crowd, both inside and out, bursts into applause. Writing again in the *New York Times*, Spindler sums up McQueen's storming of the Big Apple: "There were more ideas on this runway than in a whole season of New York shows, and he brought the level of work here up a full notch."

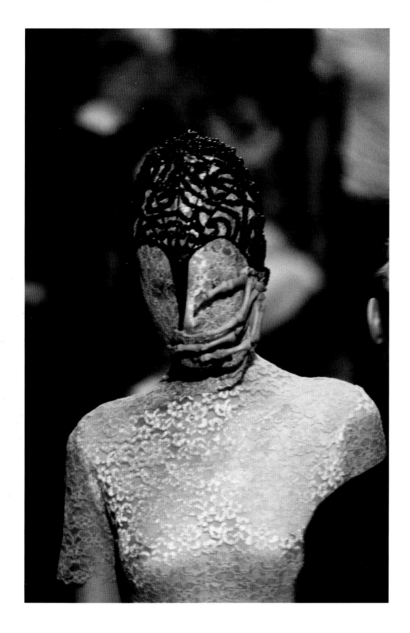

Opposite page: Is this masked model in a historically inspired top and a low-slung skirt among the saved or the damned? Her outfit seems the perfect meld of Victoriana and punk.

Above: A skeletal hand clutches the chin of a model in a lace mask.

Right: An antler headdress by Philip Treacy is worn over a coat trimmed with Mongolian fur.

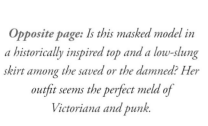

LA POUPÉE

Spring/Summer 1997

Attendance at the London fashion shows is up, and there's a

buzz about the creativity of the city. Excitement is running high.

Alexander McQueen's presentation is staged at London's Royal

Horticultural Halls. At the foot of a grand set of stairs, McQueen's

people have constructed this season's runway—a long pool of water

three inches deep. About 800 people gather around, including a

scout from Givenchy. The rumor is that McQueen may be tapped

to take over as head designer of that venerable house.

The German artist Hans Bellmer is an inspiration for this collection. Bellmer created life-size mannequins and arranged them in *tableaux vivant*, which he photographed. Some of the photographs were published in his 1932 book *Die Puppe*, which was translated into French four years later as *La Poupée*. Fashion designers have long played with the relationship between mannequins and living models, and McQueen is interested in the opportunities that dolls present for reconstructing the body and seeing it anew.

McQueen's human models descend the stairs to the flooded catwalk. With their clear platform shoes, they appear to be walking on water. Spray paint is streaked across a pink brocade jacket, a hip-hugging white skirt, and a sheer tank top. Zippers open up the knees of pants and cross the bust of tops, with the tongues hanging suggestively over the nipples. The exaggerated points of a tailored white frock coat stick out at the sides of the hips. And there are bumster trousers in a delicate pink pattern, a silver dress with a fringe skirt, and shot-silk suits.

Above: The metal circle around this model's head bobs gently over a coat with origami-like points.

Right: In addition to severe headgear by Dai Rees, this model wears a translucent overdress adorned with a fish swimming upward through swirls of blue.

Opposite page: Porcupine quills painted in glittery pink complement beautifully cut satin pants.

A model loses a shoe on her way back up the stairs, and the shoe languishes on its side. The fierce body jewelry by Dai Rees is not so easy to escape. One model's face is caged by two curved spikes that cross over her nose. The leather harness that holds them bears three more spikes that sprout like a goatee from the chin. Other models' heads are encased in glittering porcupine quills. Many of the looks are shocking—both hideous and beautiful at the same time.

Debra Shaw, her arms connected to her thighs by a metal frame, makes her halting way down the stairs and into the water (page 42). She moves in a slow dance, gesturing with her hands, the beaded fringe of her outfit swaying with her movements. People in the crowd cringe. Many are aghast to see an African-American woman so bound. Once again, a McQueen presentation excites controversy while the clothes garner positive reviews. The crowd of spectators rises in a standing ovation.

Writing in London's *Times*, Iain R. Webb summarizes this season's London Fashion Week: "There are few more rebellious, or far-sighted, than Alexander McQueen. His show was the highlight of the event." In the *New York Times*, Amy M. Spindler notes that McQueen's shock tactics aside, "the standing ovation was for the work, so sculptured and so precisely cut, that when Mr. McQueen sent the models splashing their clothes through a 50-foot wading pool that acted as a runway, it was like seeing the 'Guernica' damaged."

IT'S A JUNGLE OUT THERE

Fall/Winter 1997–98

It's February 1997, and Alexander McQueen is flying high. Last year, he was named British Designer of the Year and appointed head designer at Givenchy. The January presentation of his first Givenchy haute couture collection garnered disappointing reviews, but with no time to stew, he zipped back to London to work on the upcoming show for his own label. The invitation depicts a woman with hooves. Horns sprout from her breast and hip. A thousand people descend on a glass-roofed produce warehouse near London Bridge. Inside is a pile of derelict cars lit by flaming buckets. The crowd surges, a bucket tips over, and a car ignites.

Because the press has not arrived from the main London Fashion Week venue at the Natural History Museum, the show is delayed. When the journalists do arrive, many are unable to squeeze through the crowd and find seats. Finally, the show begins—two hours late. As the lights go down, a woman in a trench coat zigzags across the catwalk as if dodging bullets. Is she part of the show, a member of the press, or a spectator jockeying for position?

Techno music blares, and the first model appears in a black leather dress slashed open at the shoulders. Chains hang from a piece of metal that swoops down both sides of her head, covering her cheekbones. Eye makeup is black and patterned on the markings of gazelles. Many of the models, however, seem more predator than prey. They wear wild hair, animal skins, perforated leather tops, skirts, and dresses. Some wear harnesses, and some sport menacingly long silver claws.

An immaculate gray pants suit—a perfect office look—is shown with a black leather harness on top. The model's bushy hair sweeps up into two horns. A model in a sleeveless black leather top and skirt wears black fingerless gloves. When she reaches the end of the catwalk, she caresses her posterior and rocks her hips. Another model in a tailored gray jacket wears matching fur-trimmed briefs. At the end of the catwalk, she holds her breasts in her hands and leers at the audience.

A pony-skin dress in white and tan is perforated with a floral pattern. The model wears the dress with matching pony-skin boots and long silver claws on the index and little finger of her right hand (page 46). She poses, bending her knees and drawing her claws suggestively up her body. Trousers are crafted from Prince of Wales check and pony skin. Perfect McQueen jackets bear images of Old Master paintings, while others are embroidered with roses. Long curved horns sprout from the shoulders of a jacket. After the last model walks, they all take one more turn before marching out like a herd to thunderous applause.

In the *New York Times*, Amy M. Spindler says McQueen "isn't just part of the London scene; he is the scene." And, in the *Guardian*, Susannah Frankel proclaims that McQueen's "is a name that will make fashion history."

Opposite page: This form-fitting black leather dress is enhanced with embroidery down the front.

Right, top: McQueen has long found inspiration in Old Master paintings, such as the one printed on this strong-shouldered jacket.

Right, bottom: Padded shoulders make this pony-skin jacket look sharp, while the horns give it a twist of menace.

UNTITLED

Spring/Summer 1998

Word is that Alexander McQueen has been calling this show "The Golden Shower," but when American Express, his new show underwriter, realized the implications, they refused to let him use it. The invitation is made of yellow acrylic. The venue is a garage near London's Victoria Station. About a hundred people without invitations crowd the entrance, desperate to get in. Those holding the golden tickets trot up the curving concrete ramp. Banks of seats surround a runway of acrylic tanks filled with water and lit from below. On the powerful sound system, thunder crashes, sending vibrations through the hall.

The show is said to cost 70,000 pounds, and American Express is footing about half the bill. They hope that their association with the designer will help them shed their image of elite conservatism. The company is launching a new gold credit card, and they want to get the word out to the young and the hip. The company has also commissioned McQueen to design a gold suit to be premiered on the catwalk.

The lights flash like lightning, and the first model steps out in a white jacket with a scoop front and peaked shoulders. Suits are pieced together in a marquetry of pinstripes and Prince of Wales check. A tailored pinstripe jacket is shown over a snakeskin skirt. A skintight yellow snakeskin dress spirals around the model. Sheer and translucent fabric, draped strips of material, and glittery fringe reveal glimpses of breasts and buttocks.

Several of the male models are adorned with silver jawbones fitted over their chins. A female model wears an aluminum "spine" corset complete with ribcage and tail over a sparkling black dress. The lights go down, and the audience applauds. When they come back up, a muscular model in a topless white swimsuit takes the stage. The lights turn a golden yellow. Rain pours down on the catwalk, and the model dances, swinging her hips. The water in the tanks beneath her feet turns black, and the crowd cheers. From the sound system the strains of "I Can't Stand the Rain" fill the hall.

Under the golden shower, models parade in white suits and dresses. A model in a black wig gets drenched, and her dress becomes increasingly translucent (page 50). She almost appears to be topless, and black mascara tears run down her face. Kate Moss, the last model out, walks in a white muslin dress. As she leaves the stage, a slim train attached at her left hip drags through the puddles on the catwalk. Then all the models come out for a final turn, and McQueen appears. The crowd roars. Hand in hand with model Shirley Malman, who wears the American Express gold suit, McQueen takes a bow.

In the *International Herald Tribune*, Suzy Menkes writes, "It was not a ground-breaking show, in that it purified and even commercialized McQueen's essential looks, but the fabulous presentation lived up to the hype." Amy M. Spindler of the *New York Times* says of McQueen, "he played against type with a show that was mature, buoyed by theatrics that were gut-wrenching not for being disgusting but for being eloquent."

Right, top: The unusual spiral cut of this snakeskin dress makes for a body-hugging fit.

Right, bottom: Precisely pieced together, this jumpsuit of mixed fabrics hugs every curve.

Opposite page: As the model walks, the looped fringe of her top both reveals and conceals.

JOAN

Fall/Winter 1998–99

The image on the invitation—a burning face—causes some to worry.

Given Alexander McQueen's macabre bent, will the pyrotechnics be

gruesome? On the other side of a lot of parked cars, a storage building

looms—the venue for McQueen's latest show. Inside, the elevated catwalk

looks to be covered in black cinders. Spectators take seats or find standing

room in the chilly hall. On the sound system, the snap and crackle of

burning wood can be heard. A wind whips up, and the industrial lamps

hanging over the runway sway. Black curtains part, revealing a glow of

light and a bright red wall. A model steps through the gap.

This collection is named for Joan of Arc. A national hero in France and a Catholic saint, Joan was born into a peasant family in the early fifteenth century. As a young teenager, her religious visions instructed her to expel the English from France and install the Dauphin, the future Charles VII, on the French throne. Dressed as a knight, she led Charles's army to victory. Later she was captured, turned over to the English, and tried as a heretic. She was burned at the stake on May 30, 1431.

Joan has served as inspiration to many artists and writers. In terms of McQueen's work, her outsider status, persecution, and eventual martyrdom—not to mention her habit of cross-dressing—are interesting to note. Clothes as armor and clothes that look like armor come up in McQueen's collections again and again. The first model out wears a short dress of chain mail. Her blond hair is in slim braids that loop around her apparently bald head, dipping in front of her mouth. It's medieval army meets London punk.

Red contact lenses coupled with severe hair styles give the models a spooky intensity. Another chain-mail dress, this one floor length, is worn with a draped hood. Frock coats, printed with the faces of children go by. A model in black pants appears wearing actual armor. Her head and arms are covered in silver-plated metal crafted by silversmith Sarah Harmarnee. There are elegant dresses in gray, silk harem pants, sharp suits, and floor-length coats with long lines of closely placed buttons. A model stops at the end of the catwalk, brushes aside the flaps of her jacket, and with a knowing half smile, pulls up her thigh-high boots.

The lights dim. A model strides to the center of the catwalk (page 54). She wears a glittering red dress, her face and neck completely covered with a matching hood. Suddenly, flames leap from the catwalk floor, completely encircling her. Thunder roars from the sound system, and the model sways as the flames flicker. After the conflagration dies down, all the models march out. McQueen stops to kiss his mother before he takes his bow. Katy England, his stylist, joins him on the catwalk. Like his models, McQueen's hair is dyed blond and his eyes, thanks to contacts, are red.

Many in the press see signs of a new maturity. Suzy Menkes of the *International Herald Tribune* writes: "After finding fame as an aggressive agent provocateur, McQueen produced a mature and well-focused collection. Looking at the impeccable tailoring, it was hard to believe that a year ago the same designer sent out cavewoman goat skins in apocalyptic chaos." Grace Bradberry, writing in the *Times* of London, describes the burning climax of the show as "a glorious fashion image that may well sum up the whole late Nineties London thing ten years from now."

Opposite page: This floor-length dress and gracefully draped headdress make chain mail seem almost delicate.

Above: When this frock coat appears, someone in the audience says the children printed on it are the Romanovs.

Right: A model stops to pose in her silver-plated armor by Sarah Harmarnee.

NO. 13

Spring/Summer 1999

Rumor has it that the warehouse in central London, not

far from Victoria Station, used to be a storage facility

for trash. Tonight, candles perfume the air with the

scent of Magnolia grandiflora. *Two sleek robots, which*

contrast with the unvarnished wooden planks of the

floor, sit center stage on opposite sides of a circle cut into

the boards. The machines' metal parts seem folded in on

themselves. Around the stage, the seats are all full, and

a number of spectators sit on the stairs.

Alexander McQueen's inspiration for this show—his thirteenth—lies in a variety of sources, including Arts and Crafts, the design movement that was popular between 1860 and 1910. Arts and Crafts practitioners, such as William Morris, reacted against the use of machines by emphasizing handcrafting and natural forms. The designer also cites an installation by Rebecca Horn called *High Noon* (1991), in which two rifles suspended from a ceiling fire red paint at each other.

Another inspiration: Aimee Mullins, a Paralympic athlete and model, whose legs were amputated below the knee when she was just a year old, wears prosthetics. As guest editor of *Dazed & Confused*, McQueen featured her in the September 1998 issue, where she appears as both a fragile doll and a strong, fierce, almost superhuman athlete. The issue of the magazine, which was titled "Fashion-Able," included eight differently abled models, a number of whom are attending tonight's show.

The stage is flooded with blue light. Aimee Mullins strides out, swinging her arms. Her intricately carved "boots" are, in fact, prosthetic legs that were designed by McQueen and handcrafted over five weeks by the Dorset Orthopaedic Company. The wooden prosthetics are decorated with vines and flowers in keeping with the Arts and Crafts tradition. There are frock coats worn with a cropped version of McQueen's bumster trousers, skirts and dresses with asymmetrical hems, one-shouldered tunics, and off-the-shoulder tops that bind the upper arms to the sides. One of these is worn over a skirt made of mirrored tiles, like a disco ball.

A Regency-stripe top with a high collar is worn over a semi-sheer floor-length skirt ending in narrow tiers of ruffles. Then there's a dress of delicate green lace—but with a twist. Instead of being soft, this lace is stiff enough to stand up on its own. Traditional-looking trousers have a surprise at the rear— an inverted jacket, sleeves and all, hangs from the back of the waist. A black-haired model in a top with fanlike balsa-wood wings is followed by variations on earlier looks: tops, skirts, and dresses embellished with ruffles and lace, and more beautifully tailored suits.

The lights dim, and two models appear, rotating on discs built into the stage. They wear intricately carved balsa-wood skirts that splay out like sandalwood fans. The lights come up, and more suits, skirts, and dresses go by. A lace dress is worn with a leather neckpiece—like the corset Mullins wears in her second turn (page 58), it looks like a medical device from a previous century.

The lights go down again, and spotlights pick out five models spinning like jewelry-box dolls in glittery crystal-studded costumes. As they leave the stage, the lights come up on models wearing white skirts, pants, and dresses with lace insets that show flashes of skin. Then there is a stunning sheer white frock coat embroidered with long-necked birds, butterflies, and flowers.

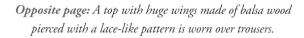

Opposite page: A top with huge wings made of balsa wood pierced with a lace-like pattern is worn over trousers.

Above: Echoing a technique often used by Arts and Crafts practitioners to draw attention to their workmanship, McQueen left the edges of this sleeveless top unfinished and frayed to contrast with the precision of the finished seams.

Right: A collaborative effort of McQueen, milliner Philip Treacy, and jeweler Shaun Leane, the spiral swirl around this model glitters with Swarovski crystals.

The lights lower and come up again. Model Shalom Harlow stands in the circle cut into the floor at center stage. The circle begins to turn. From the front, her strapless white dress looks a bit like a full skirt that's been pulled up above the bust and fastened with a thick leather belt. The audience begins to applaud. The two robots raise their snouts and peer at Harlow, who lifts one hand as if to ward them off. The machines flex their snaky necks, following the model's doll-like movements. One robot zeros in on her skirt and fires black paint over the pure white fabric. Harlow holds her head in dismay, and the other machine lets loose with a spray of acid yellow.

Like the machines that artist Rebecca Horn uses in her installations, such as the paint-firing rifles that inspired McQueen, these robots seem to have emotions. Are they somewhat human? And if they are, then what are we? The platform continues to rotate as the machines cover Harlow's dress with paint. The audience continues to applaud. Then the robots are done. They raise their heads, turn away from Harlow, and seem to bow to the audience before sinking back to the stage. Harlow's platform stops rotating, and she staggers off to cheers from the crowd.

In the *International Herald Tribune*, Suzy Menkes writes, "McQueen staged the triumph of London's fashion week." She continues, "McQueen captured the raw aggression of Britpop and the swaggering showmanship of the art scene," and concludes her review of McQueen's show with "The sheer volume of ideas and their fine execution . . . was breathtaking."

Robots spray Shalom Harlow's dress with black and yellow paint as she balances on a slowly revolving turntable cut into the floor.

THE OVERLOOK

Fall/Winter 1999–2000

"All work and no play makes Jack a dull boy," the invitation

reads. The sentence is repeated more than forty times. For

those familiar with Stanley Kubrick's horror film The Shining

(1980), the spine begins to tingle. This is what Jack Nicholson's

character types over and over again—after he has lost his mind.

Attendees are warned to dress warmly, and they arrive at the

venue for Alexander McQueen's show in Victoria, Central

London, in boots and extra sweaters. A few carry blankets.

The building—some say it serves as overnight parking for garbage trucks—is dark. Inside are candles and a giant Plexiglass cube encapsulating a winter wonderland of white birch trees and snow. "The Overlook" is named after the hotel in Kubrick's classic film. McQueen draws not from the blood-soaked plot of the film, but from the setting—the isolated, snowbound, haunted hotel inhabited by the ill-fated Torrance family in the off-season.

A howling wind and the occasional baying of wolves can be heard over the sound system. Cate Blanchett, Grace Jones, Helen Mirren, and Kate Winslett settle into their seats. McQueen plans to show in New York next season, and people already worry what London Fashion Week will be like without him. But McQueen has promised "The Overlook" will be his best show yet. The venue certainly has edgy atmosphere. Electronic dance music starts, and the first model enters the cube.

The first outfits are black with high necks and elongated torsos. The models pose, some of them stopping at the wall of the cube, placing their hands on the barrier, and gazing out. There are knits and long frock coats with asymmetrical tails, semi-sheer floor-length skirts, and sumptuous furs, including a mid-calf rabbit-fur skirt. A sleeveless tan leather dress with a long waist and extra-high collar is painted with roses. Puffer jackets, both cropped and with long tails, and Icelandic-style jackets—leather with fur on the inside—in browns and taupe go by, then a suede dress, the fur within peeking out at the seams and hem.

Two red-haired models in identical gray outfits walk with intertwined arms and give the Kubrick fans in the audience a jolt. The two women recall the Grady girls, the ghosts of murdered sisters who haunt young Danny Torrance in *The Shining*, chanting "Come and play with us, Danny. Forever . . . and ever . . . and ever." Next come razor-sharp suits with typical McQueen embellishments: long tails and cutaway jackets. A model wearing an elegant black coat with a dropped waist goes by, and the wolves howl to rap music and the cawing of birds.

Left: The identical outfits and intertwined arms of these models spook the audience by invoking the Grady girls from Stanley Kubrick's The Shining.

Above: The "Coiled" Corset of aluminum wire by Shaun Leane for Alexander McQueen is worn with a soft gray wool puff skirt and "skating" shoes.

A metal corset with a high neck fabricated by Shaun Leane is inspired by the coiled necklaces of indigenous South African people. For an exact fit, the model's body was cast in concrete, then each coil was wound around the form by hand. A screwdriver is required to get in and out of the corset, which fastens along the sides. A long flannel skirt with delicate cut-out decorations is followed by a ballet crinoline in filigreed metal. A real showpiece, the skirt is reflective, sending out its own beams of light.

Right: *The Petrouschka skirt, this season's ballet crinoline, is shown here in cut metal.*

The lights fade. They come up again, and an ice skater dressed all in white sails out into the cube, followed by six more skaters (page 64). She is joined by six more skaters. The strains of a big band tune play as the skaters dance across the ice, circling and spinning, their skirts fanning out around them. Al Bowlly sings "Midnight, the Stars, and You," a romantic song that took on an undertone of terror after Kubrick used it in *The Shining*. The ice dance finishes, and the skaters depart.

A wolf howls. Inside the cube, a wind whips up, blowing thick snow through the air. A model encased in glittering crystals, as if she is a snowflake or an Arctic sprite, emerges from a cloud of snow. There are white versions of the earlier-seen black coats, cable-knit sweaters, and stiff lacy skirts. A strapless dress of rabbit fur embroidered with flowers goes by. A model in a lace dress adorned with crystals raises her arms, places her hands on her head, and opens her mouth, as if she, like the wolves, feels the need to bay at the moon. She holds her arms out, open to the elements, and the lights go down.

McQueen gets a standing ovation. Members of the audience are in tears. He has so clearly given the best of himself. In the *International Herald Tribune*, Suzy Menkes writes that McQueen is an international talent who has electrified London Fashion Week. She goes on: "For its light-handed workmanship and intense imagination, this show was, for McQueen, a shining moment."

"*[The show] was about the sense of isolation and obscurity . . . it was the romantic side of the film.*"

—Alexander McQueen

Opposite page: *A model wears a rock-crystal bodice by Kees van der Graaf for Alexander McQueen.*

Right: *Swarovski crystals give this high-necked lace dress its all-over sparkle.*

EYE

Spring/Summer 2000

This season, Alexander McQueen is staging his first major show in New York, and it may be the most anticipated fashion event of the year. Rumors about the show abound: Some say he plans to suspend models from the Brooklyn Bridge. Others say he's going to use 240 models, that they will walk through a pool of oil, and that the show will cost a million dollars. The location is kept secret until the last minute. To add to the drama, a hurricane is heading up the coast. New York's mayor issues an order for schools and businesses to close and for people to return home by three in the afternoon.

Although many shows have been cancelled, McQueen's evening presentation at Pier 94 on the Hudson River is on. More than a thousand people brave the torrential rain and gusting sixty-mile-per-hour winds to attend. Inside the cavernous warehouse is a shallow pool. The music starts, and the first model strides out, splashing through the water and sending up droplets that glisten in the spotlight.

She wears a black coat drenched with white embroidery and nothing underneath. The extra-long sleeves are slit open from the elbow to the wrist. When she poses with her hands on her hips at the end of the runway, the sleeves hang down like elegant bells. The next model peers out over a black veil worn with a typically sharp McQueen pantsuit, also in black. Long ribbons extending from the veil flutter around her legs as she walks.

This show is said to be a protest against the repression of Islamic women, with the water on the runway representing the oil of wealthy middle-eastern countries. In keeping with the Islamic theme, veils appear along with crescent moon motifs—but the designs are counterbalanced by a western sensibility; McQueen alternately hides and reveals the body. There are jumpsuits with super-low waistlines that elongate the torso, harem pants, and leather bathing suits that mask the face and bare the breast. Red and white striped pantaloons, silky athletic shorts, and college-style T-shirts go by. A model in red boxer shorts and a long cape that drags in the water behind her walks off, and the lights dim.

The music swells. Metal spikes rise from the water. Ten feet above the spikes, a black-clad figure sitting cross-legged floats toward the audience, her hands resting in the jnana mudra position, palms upward on her knees (page 70). The scene, lit by intermittently flashing spotlights, seems to incorporate elements drawn from early Hinduism and Buddhism as well as Islam. More aerialists in robes swoop out, moving their legs as if trying to run. Another turns graceful somersaults as she moves through the air. Two more hang motionless—then start to twitch as though being electrocuted. As the show ends, McQueen takes a bow amid the catwalk's metal spikes and pulls down his jeans to reveal a pair of boxers bearing the stars and stripes.

Reception to the show is mixed. Many feel McQueen has overdone the theatrics. In the *International Herald Tribune*, Suzy Menkes writes, "McQueen has infused modern romance with bravura staging in his recent London shows, but in the hard-edged New York presentation, he missed the magical fusion of function and fantasy."

Opposite page: One model's face is hidden by a hooded top of jeweled armor worn over a bikini bottom.

Right, top: Worn over a sleeveless college athletic top featuring stars and crescent moons, a body ornament by Reena Ahluwalia is studded with 2,409 diamonds.

Right, bottom: Opulent embroidery and extra-long slit-open sleeves set this jacket apart.

ESHU

Fall/Winter 2000–01

After showing his eponymous label in New York last season, Alexander McQueen is debuting his fall/winter collection in the city of his birth. The London fashion world lets out a collective sigh of relief. Their bad boy and rising commercial star has not abandoned them. And McQueen's star and visibility continue to rise: an Alexander McQueen corset is on display at a museum in New York, and McQueen is working on a video with rapper Lil' Kim. About two weeks before the presentation of his collection, he tells the Times *of London that his show preparations include blowing up a building with dynamite.*

The show is named for Eshu, the trickster god of the Yoruba people of West Africa. Eshu likes to test mortals and often sows discord as a way to teach. He is also a messenger, the protector of travelers, and a lover of dogs. Perhaps it is this association that has caused an attempted sabotage of McQueen's runway show. Animal rights activists are said to have broken into the venue and vandalized the set with red paint.

In a steady drizzle, spectators arrive at the old Gainsborough Studios in Hoxton, East London, the site where Alfred Hitchcock filmed his early thrillers, to find more police than protestors. Security guards inspect the bags of all the guests and hold up the show's starting time by an hour. A rumor is going around that there's been a bomb threat. Inside, the building seems derelict. Shards of broken slate cover the catwalk.

Finally, the spectators are seated. Drumming comes from the soundtrack as a model descends a long sloping gangway that runs along three sides of the huge room. As she steps gingerly onto the rocky catwalk, the crowd begins to applaud. She wears a full-face mask with a bushy mane (page 74). Her dress, with its leg-of-mutton sleeves, would suit a Victorian lady but for the clay smeared over the skirt. Next comes a precisely tailored white wool coat, also bearing a layer of dried clay. On the models' heads, a wide stripe of bright yellow paint that runs from forehead to crown shines in the lights.

A leather dress with a lacy cutout design is supported by a visible metal crinoline. Another has a hem that appears to have been cut with pinking shears. Chunky white knits seem to bubble up around the faces of two models. Narrow strips cut into the back of a bodice undulate like fringe. Densely packed fabric roses seem to smother a model in a chocolate brown ensemble, covering her breasts and shoulders and inching up toward her ears. On another ensemble, the roses cover the skirt, which is worn with a shaped corset that rises from the hips to the neck.

As the show progresses, the jewelry becomes extreme—giant earrings of concentric hoops, loosely coiled neck rings, an orthodontic-looking device that pulls one model's lips into a painful-looking rictus. A model in a black floor-length coat of wavy synthetic hair, two models wearing sheer black gossamer dresses, one dotted with sparkling crystals, another model in a black satin dress with a skirt that stands out stiffly from the body, and the show is over.

The fashion press is mostly positive, although Ginia Bellafante of the *New York Times* concludes that the discomfort borne by the models "almost eclipsed the exceptional" clothes in the show. But McQueen is skewered in the popular press, which runs headlines: "The Designer Who Hates Women" and "It's time to give these fashion freaks the bum's rush." Could Eshu be at work here, too?

Opposite page: The artfully uneven hem of a leather dress rises high to reveal the metal crinoline that supports it.

Left: Neck rings and bars that seem to pierce the nose are among the extreme jewelry shown in this collection.

Above: On the back of a bodice made with strips of fabric that sway with the model's movements, Wanda Wulz's 1932 photo of a woman's face merging with the whiskered muzzle of a cat flickers in and out of focus.

VOSS

Spring/Summer 2001

The venue is an old bus depot near London's Thames River. Amid rumors that Alexander McQueen is unhappy at Givenchy, his team has been working on the set for his own label's show all week. Security at the depot is tight. Inside, a giant mirrored cube greets those lucky enough to gain entrance. Of the eighty shows this week, McQueen's is the one to see. The audience settles in and waits, some staring at their own reflections, others looking away. Apparently Gwyneth Paltrow is stuck in traffic; the show will begin once she arrives. On the soundtrack, an eerily amplified heartbeat. The audience grows impatient.

Victorian depictions of madness gave McQueen much of the inspiration for this show. He also drew on New Mexico–based photographer Joel-Peter Witkin's *Sanitarium* (1983), which pictures a large naked woman reclining. Small wings sprout from the sides of her head, and she seems to breathe through a tube in her mouth. McQueen also found a fecund source in *The Green Mile* (1999), a film about a 1930s prison guard on death row who witnessed supernatural events.

The music starts, and the house lights dim. Lights come up in the cube, which is now mirrored on the inside. The unmirrored walls are padded, and the catwalk floor is tiled in white: a cell in an asylum for the insane. In the center looms a huge box with stained sides. Kate Moss, with a tightly bandaged head as if she has recently undergone surgery or perhaps been treated with electroshock, lurches into the space, presses her hands against the mirrored walls, and gazes at her own reflection.

*"The [razor-clam]
shells had outlived their
usefulness on the beach,
so we put them to another
use on the dress. Then Erin
came out and trashed the
dress, so their usefulness
was over once again. Kind
of like fashion, really."*

—Alexander McQueen

In her ruffled pink dress and buff-colored mules with metal heels that are so thin they're almost invisible, Moss presses off and launches herself at another wall. Stella Tennant, her head also bandaged, wears an elegant black slip dress that seems to have a feather boa sprouting from one side. Another model's arms are pinned down by an embroidered coat—or could it be an unusually elegant straightjacket?

Jade Parfitt, in a floor-length ostrich-feather skirt and loose silk top, has a flock of predatory birds arrayed around her head, pulling at the fabric of her blouse (page 78). Another model wears a bell-shaped dress of green ostrich feathers under a sleeveless coat with a thermal image of McQueen's face printed on the back. The lights turn blue as Erin O'Connor walks out in a floor-length dress of razor-clam shells. She leans her head back and grabs handfuls of shells, breaking them and dropping the fragments to the floor.

Opposite page: Erin O'Connor models
a dress made of stripped and varnished
razor-clam shells.

Left: A bright green ostrich-feather dress
bursts the confines of a narrow silk coat.

Above: An embroidered hat looks more
like a flower box with its decoration
of trailing Amaranthus.

A model wearing a partially completed jigsaw puzzle as a top is followed by Roos van Bosstraeten with a miniature sandcastle perched on her left shoulder. Amy Wesson, her mussel-shell skirt dragging on the floor behind her, stops with a look of mad frustration, grabs her skirt and shakes it, sending shells crashing to the floor. There are chic and wearable suits in gray, pink, and pale blue, silk jersey dresses, and long-sleeved pastel shirts worn with matching ties. Appliquéd flower roundels cover a high-collared coat, skirt, and gown.

Karen Elson's overdress, constructed from the panels of a nineteenth-century Japanese screen, is worn over a dress made of overlapping oyster shells. When she poses by the mirrored glass, she nibbles at the points of her silver neckpiece by Shaun Leane. Erin O'Connor appears again, this time wearing a gown made of glass microscope slides and feathers. She leans against the big box in the center of the cube, pushes off, and is gone.

Opposite page: Appliqués of silk-embroidered roundels in the shape of chrysanthemums cover this floor-sweeping dress with a skirt of black ostrich feathers.

Left: Erin O'Connor's dress has a top made of glass microscope slides painted red to indicate blood, and a skirt of red and black ostrich feathers.

Above: The image of a castle decorates the jigsaw-puzzle top of one model, while behind her, Roos van Bosstraeten wears a small castle on one shoulder.

"*It was about trying to trap something that wasn't conventionally beautiful to show that beauty comes from within.*"

—Alexander McQueen

The stage is dark. Then a spotlight shines down on one side of the large stained box. As the lights come up, the glass walls of the box break away from the metal frame and fall, shattering. Inside, a naked woman reclines, a tube sprouting from her mouth. Moths and butterflies swarm around her. McQueen has brought Witkin's photograph to life. The heartbeat on the soundtrack stops, replaced by the steady tone of a flat-line alarm.

The audience is rapt, as if they have been watching a gorgeous horror film. The applause is thunderous, and the critics are wowed. "In terms of both imagination and execution, McQueen is simply miles ahead of the pack," writes Jess Cartner-Morley, fashion editor of the *Guardian*. Cathy Horyn in the *New York Times* notes that McQueen is "responding, like an artist, to the horror and insanity in contemporary culture." Suzy Menkes of the *International Herald Tribune* writes: "This was McQueen, now trained in Paris couture, at his most discreetly inventive. No flash, no aggression, only luxurious calm."

McQueen has created a tableau vivant *of Joel-Peter Witkin's photograph* Sanitarium *(1983).*

WHAT A MERRY-GO-ROUND

Fall/Winter 2001–02

Again this season, Alexander McQueen's show is held in the disused bus depot in London's SW1. And again, security is fierce. A crowd of fashion students argue, angling to get in. Last night, McQueen was named Designer of the Year at the British Fashion Awards. Although still employed by Givenchy, McQueen sold 51 percent of his eponymous label to the Gucci Group in December. All of which, coupled with McQueen's reputation for great showmanship, means that this is the show everyone's been waiting for. The lucky few who have invitations are herded into a waiting area more like a holding pen, and they wait and wait.

Once inside, the spectators, who include Kate Moss, Bianca Jagger, and Domenico de Sole, CEO of the Gucci Group—in effect, McQueen's new boss—cram themselves into seats. In the center of the stage, an antique carousel turns. The horses are sheathed in purple, lavender, and black latex. A large spiral of gray and blue is painted on the catwalk floor. When the lights come up, it still seems dark.

Over the sound system comes the creepy voice of the child catcher from the 1968 movie *Chitty Chitty Bang Bang*, enticing unwary tots with promises of free candy and ice cream. Then the loudspeakers thunder with Marilyn Manson–style rock. The first looks out are military. Hair is marcelled into curls, and the models wear dark lipstick. The styling suggests pre-war Germany, the look of the musical *Cabaret*.

The feeling is decadent. The models strut out to the blaring music, then twirl around poles that rise from the floor. Several small airplanes seem to have crashed into the head of one model in a military-style suit with high boots. Other models wear caramel-colored leather—a coat cut to look like fish scales, a suit with a sleeveless jacket, a body-skimming knee-length dress. A model in a long, belted white coat trimmed with gold braid stops to glare at the audience. Following her are several models in silky jersey dresses that cling to the figure.

For evening, McQueen has created dashing Asian-style embroidered wrap jackets with dramatically high asymmetrical collars. Marleen Berkova wears an elegant tuxedo-style coatdress that wraps smoothly around her body. On her shoulders, instead of a fur piece, she wears the skeleton of a small animal. Natasa Vojnovic, in a leather jacket, a miniskirt of peacock feathers, and high, dangerously pointy boots, sticks out her tongue and licks her lips lasciviously. She prances up to a pole, straddles it, and dances suggestively, gyrating her hips.

A moiré suit with an oversize jacket and a fur coat with an asymmetrical hem are followed by long lacy see-through dresses sparkling with crystals. A gown with a peacock-feather top and long leather skirt with a cutout design, more outfits in shiny leather—including a floor-length black coat worn with a military hat sporting huge feather plumes—and an unraveling sweaterdress with the image of a skull and crossbones on the front, and the lights go down.

Opposite page: This wrap coat of black silk is embroidered with gold bullion thread.

Above: Natasa Vojnovic plays the part of a bad girl in leather and a feather skirt.

Right: A delicate see-through dress is worn with a black leather helmet by Philip Treacy for Alexander McQueen. The headpiece is trimmed with black pearls, ostrich feathers, and a skull pierced by a dagger.

A curtain at the back of the stage rises to reveal an attic of abandoned toys—rocking horses and bobbling dolls, ventriloquists' dummies, giant teddy bears, and a huge bunch of black and orange balloons. From this tableau, clowns rise, clowns in fright wigs and elegant evening gowns. Over the sound system comes an eerie serenade, the theme from the film *Rosemary's Baby* (1968). The balloons, it turns out, are all attached to the wide ruffled skirt of a single clown. With difficulty, pushing the balloons out of her way, she slowly walks to the center of the carousel. Two more clowns, holding scissors aloft, follow her. They cut the strings of the balloons and release them into the air. Yet another clown walks toward the audience, dragging a golden human skeleton (page 86).

The clowns on the merry-go-round watch the models parade in their final turn to the strains of "A Spoonful of Sugar." McQueen comes out and stops to shake hands with De Sole, who looks ecstatic. In his baggy jeans and floppy shirt, the designer takes a quick walk around the carousel. On his way backstage, he grabs the retreating feet of the last model's golden skeleton and carries it off, giving a flirty little backward kick with one foot.

As far as the spectators and some members of the press are concerned, the show is a success. Hilary Alexander of London's *Daily Telegraph* writes, "Despite the theatrics and the air of angry unease, this was a strong show of commercial clothes." There is some criticism, though. Suzy Menkes of the *International Herald Tribune* points out that McQueen has "mapped out no new territory" but instead has simply "refined his signature looks."

In the grand finale, clowns clad in evening wear ride the slowly turning carousel.

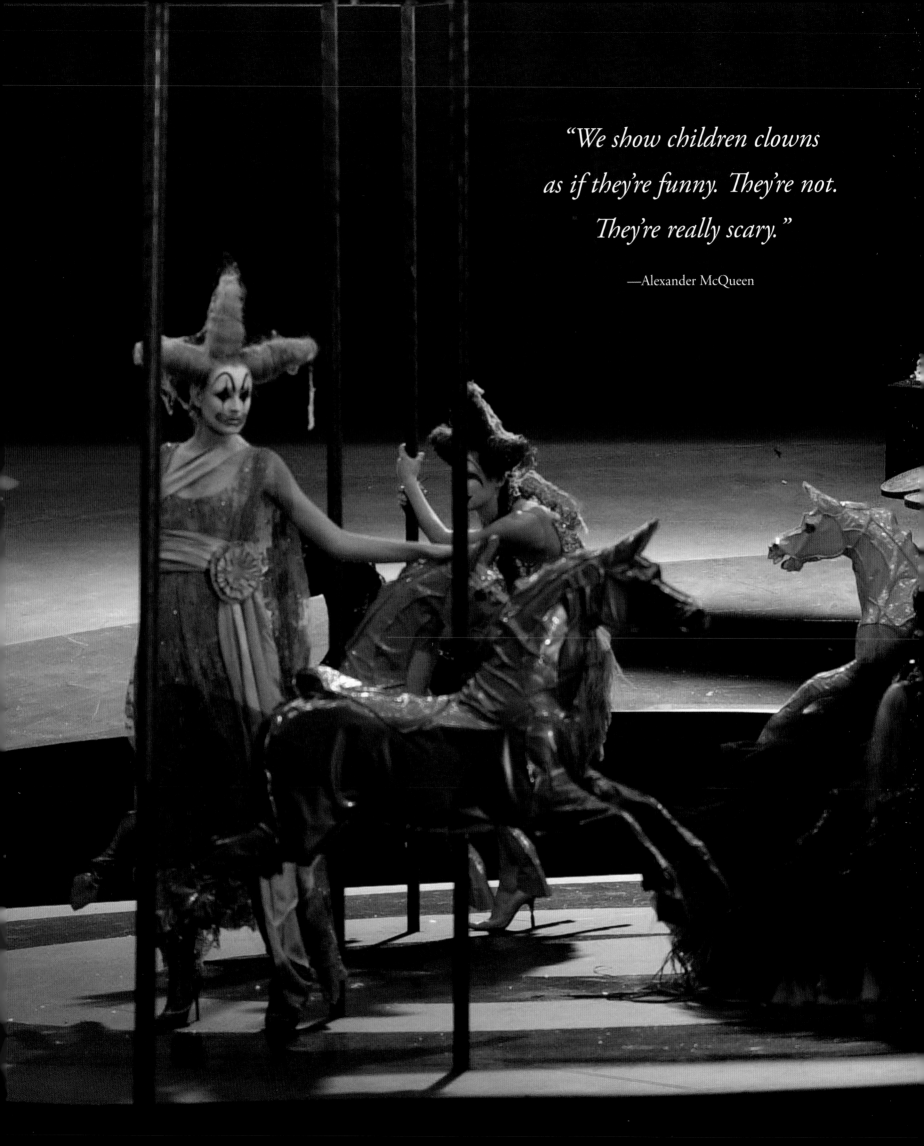

"*We show children clowns as if they're funny. They're not. They're really scary.*"

—Alexander McQueen

THE DANCE OF
THE TWISTED BULL

Spring/Summer 2002

Pierced with holes, the blood-red invitation to the Alexander McQueen label's

first Paris outing depicts a gored bull taking its last breaths. It's a rainy Saturday

night, with fog, less than a month after the September 11, 2001, terrorist

attacks on New York and Washington. Security at the show is especially tight.

The audience settles down in the pitch-dark auditorium. Dry ice "smoke" billows

down from a ledge above the stage. There's the percussive sound of Spanish

dancing as the projection of a larger-than-life matador, beating out a rhythm

with his feet, appears behind the wall of smoke.

Matadors and flamenco dancers have inspired this collection, which plays with the notion of masculinity versus femininity, the sharp and the crisp versus lace and ruffles, tailored suits versus chiffon dresses. Here, too, are the familiar McQueen themes of sex and death coupled with his signature dark romanticism. McQueen presented his final collection for Givenchy in March. This is his first show produced in partnership with the Gucci Group.

The screen matador swishes his red cape, and the first models stride out from the wall of smoke. Three of them, clad all in gray, walk abreast, the image of a bull looming behind them. The dresses are cut out on the sides and at the front so that they resemble harnesses. They're followed by wearable-looking pants, also in gray, shown with low-slung belts and barely there harness tops. Carmen Maria Hillestad and Mini Andén wear simply tailored off-the-shoulder dresses with partially poufed skirts, one white, one gray.

Mariacarla Boscono, in an all-white ensemble, seems both feminine and masculine at the same time, epitomizing McQueen's gender play. Karolina Kurkova takes a turn in a black-and-white dress that explodes in polka-dot ruffles cascading down one side from shoulder to floor. Exquisitely tailored suits go by, some, in matador style, worn with bicorn hats. In the background, smoke continues to billow as the bullfight goes on. White ensembles with skirts of eyelet lace are followed by a gray suit. The tiered skirt with its tiny pierced pattern looks as if it was made from a Spanish fan. Abbey Shaine comes out covered in large structured ruffles that run from her mermaid skirt all the way up the back of her beige dress.

Laura Morgan wears a red and white ruffled dress pierced with spears that seem to impale her while holding up her long train (page 92). There are skinny striped pants that could be worn by most anyone anywhere. Cutouts on the sides of a slinky black dress reveal the model's jutting hipbones. Long ribbons, which wrap harness-like around waists and midriffs, dangle down and flutter around the models' legs. The back of a black suit is unexpectedly draped with what looks like a matador's cape. Skimpy polka-dot slip dresses, some bound with leather straps, go by. Suave, sophisticated, and triumphant, Luciana Marinessen takes the last turn in a black matador-style suit. To the sound of moaning, a woman's face in the throes of sex appears on the screen. Her expression becomes one of terror. A sword slices the air, and the billowing smoke turns blood red. The models storm out like a herd to take their final turn. McQueen, in jeans and a sleeveless vest, comes out, waves, and ducks back into the smoke.

Some spectators object to the moaning sounds, others to the violent sexual imagery. Cathy Horyn of the *New York Times* feels the show is overwrought. Robin Givhan of the *Washington Post* writes, "McQueen was at his best when he worked his tailoring magic; his dressmaking flourishes were too showy and indulgent."

Right, top: Wearing this powerful look, Mariacarla Boscono could take down any bull.

Right, bottom: Luciana Marinissen, the last model to walk, shows off her matador style in a jacket covered with intricate jet beading.

Opposite page: Polka dots in a variety of combinations— red dots on a black ground, black dots on red, black dots on white—are a featured pattern in this collection.

SUPERCALI-FRAGILISTICEX-PIALIDOCIOUS

Fall/Winter 2002–03

The invitation to Alexander McQueen's latest show takes the form of a school notebook. Inside, illustrations of women in asymmetrical dresses share the page with artfully splotchy inkblots. The drawings are by film director and producer Tim Burton. The last page of the notebook reads "and the show begins howling!!!" The venue is the Conciergerie, a former palace and prison that contains the cell where Marie Antoinette spent her last night on Earth. The dimly lit hall is full of vaulted archways. Barred windows open on to the galleries above, and dark shadows prowl the groined ceiling.

The title of the show comes from the 1964 film *Mary Poppins*. There are references to Grimms' fairy tales as well as schoolgirls gone bad, strict schoolmistresses, S&M, swashbuckling highwaymen, and lovely princesses. The music is from Tim Burton's *Sleepy Hollow* (1999), a film retelling of the legend of the headless horseman. It all adds up to a dark romantic fantasy, one with lots of stunning clothes.

A blue-tinted spotlight comes on, creating a bright path. A woman in a lilac hooded jacket appears, leading two wolves. They walk in a large square, passing under historic archways. As they approach a wall, the upstairs is illuminated, and the ominous shadows prove to be those of more wolves—a pack of them, pacing back and forth in their cell. Little Lilac Riding Hood walks off, and the next model takes her turn. The fairy-tale journey is underway.

The first looks are impeccably tailored tweed—a McQueen signature. These are shown with tall lace-up boots and harnesses that buckle at the waist and under the bust. There's denim, too—jeans, a dress, a slim jumpsuit. Hair is worn in three pigtails wrapped in fabric. Light from the gallery casts the shadows of bars on the floor.

Dresses and skirts in rich burgundy leather are next. They feature ruched chiffon at the neckline for a touch of milkmaid softness. Roos van Bosstraeten looks ready for any type of adventure in high boots, a cape, and lingerie. Isabeli Fontana strides by in a black leather coat with strong shoulders. Then it's subverted school uniforms, each a statement of individuality. These are worn with Kiss-style makeup and bowler hats—a nod to Stanley Kubrick's *A Clockwork Orange* (1971). As Karen Elson, in an offbeat uniform, turns to pose, she lets out an exclamation of "Whoa!" Then there are evening looks, mostly in black with lace and with fringe, and delicate romantic dresses that gain toughness from leather harnesses and trim. Kamila Szczawinska, who could be a highwayman as she walks in a billowing silk cape and shiny hip-hugging pants, is followed by Maja Latinovic, a winter princess swathed in fur. The show ends, and McQueen comes out, looking dapper in a Savile Row suit, a big change from his typical jeans and T-shirt.

Hilary Alexander of London's *Daily Telegraph* writes that this collection "was spectacular, revealing a designer at ease and in love with his profession." Sarah Mower of Style.com says that with this show "Alexander McQueen proved to Paris that his design can stand on its own dramatically erotic strengths." And Susannah Frankel writes in the *Independent*: "This was McQueen's strongest collection for some time."

Right, top: Anne Vyalitsyna's shiny lace-up boots would surely garner attention from the principal.

Right, bottom: Luxurious furs will keep this princess warm no matter how cold it is outside.

Opposite page: Kamila Szczawinska wears a tricorn hat by Philip Treacy for Alexander McQueen with her highwayman outfit.

IRERE

Spring/Summer 2003

Anticipation at Alexander McQueen's new show is running high. A large crowd of 2,500 people clamor to see the theatrical fashion master's new ideas. Before the audience is a bright white stage, a white ceiling suspended above. Suddenly, the back wall is lit by the intense blue of the ocean, an underwater scene, rays of light, broken, refracted, piercing the indigo depths. The sound of waves breaking, then—a splash. A woman falls into the water. Her gown, made up of strands of trailing chiffon, swirls around her, tangling in her legs and arms like seaweed. She struggles to free herself, undulating in a watery dance. And then she is motionless: drowned, suspended eerily, and yet, still lovely. She has been transformed from simple beauty into something more layered and complex, thanks to the work of film director John Maybury.

McQueen found inspiration for this show in the 1986 Roland Joffé film *The Mission*, the story of a Spanish Jesuit who attempts to protect a South American tribe from pro-slavery Portuguese forces. The movie is based on historic events surrounding the 1750 signing of the Treaty of Madrid, which set a boundary of demarcation between the colonial territories of Spain and Portugal and led to the Guaraní War, in which thousands of indigenous people perished.

The word *Irere* is said to mean "transformation" in one of the indigenous languages of the Amazon River Basin. The story of this show, which has three distinct sections, centers on a shipwrecked woman and her journey of transformation. In the film, she is drowned. On the catwalk, she transforms from pirate to conquistador, and finally, to Amazonian princess. McQueen also cites Christopher Columbus and Captain Cook, thus inviting us to become explorers and begin our own transformative journey.

In front of the drowning woman on the screen, the models appear. Their hair is wet and their makeup smeared, as if they have just been plucked from the sea. Transformed into pirates, they strut the runway in short leather skirts, pantaloons, brocade jackets, and boots with flipped-down tops. The sharp tailoring of the jackets is softened with unraveling lace, shredded chiffon, McQueen's signature skull scarf, and a few spectacular dresses, including what is to become an iconic gown, the "Oyster" dress worn by Leticia Birkheuer (page 100). Constructed with boning and tulle on top, the dress is fabricated from hundreds of organza circles joined together and applied to the skirt in wavy overlapping lines.

On the screen, a gathering of women appears, aglow in an otherworldly green light. Their eyes burn bright through masks of black makeup. The scene shifts to a forest and the wailing and tribal music are drowned out by the song "Son of a Preacher Man." Mariacarla Boscono appears in a flouncy dress of black lace that recalls the Catholic Church, grieving widows, flamenco dancers, and the conquistadors who conquered the Aztec and Inca Empires. Like the women on the screen, the models wear black makeup masks, which only underscore their surreal beauty.

Some reviewers see this section as typical McQueen gothic, and Sarah Mower of Style.com calls the black pieces "largely redundant." But there are surprises here. Olivia Inge walks out in a glittering catsuit covered in black glass beads. Coupled with her silver face disc, crafted by Shaun Leane, and her makeup, she becomes an ancient colonizer, a dark and mysterious bird, an alien visiting Earth from a distant galaxy.

*Opposite page: Soft ruffles add
a feminine twist to Ann Oost's
pirate outfit.*

*Above: Marcelle Bittar is fierce and ready to
conquer the world in sheer pants and a sheer
embroidered cape.*

*Right: Olivia Inge wears a bodysuit of
nude silk embroidered with black glass beads
and a face disc by Shaun Leane for
Alexander McQueen.*

On the screen, the images shift again. A woman, rendered in the wild colors of heat-sensitive film—her face red, hair and body blue—approaches. The percussive sound of rattles, a bird call, and Linda Vojtova appears on the runway in a flowing blue and white dress and tribal jewelry, a feathered bone though her nose. Each Amazon-inspired outfit is more colorful than the last. Swirling tie-dyed dresses flounce above Lucite heels containing real butterflies. Feathers proliferate as headdresses, earrings, and brightly colored bolero jackets. The vibrant hues are unexpected and stunning. Cathy Horyn of the *New York Times* writes, "Mr. McQueen's brilliant stroke was to connect the past and present through the triumph of nature—in tropical paradise colors that now spread, like a drug-induced haze, on fluttery chiffon dresses." Even after the show is over, the excitement, the color-soaked fluttering continues.

Opposite page: Erika Wall's ensemble mixes a classically tailored jacket—typical McQueen— with one of his new rain forest–inspired prints.

Right: Yasmin Warsame is the picture of an Amazonian princess in a colorful feather headdress by Philip Treacy for Alexander McQueen.

SCANNERS

Fall/Winter 2003–04

The invitations to this show bear images of a brain scan, and the brain is Alexander McQueen's. His company is about to open a flagship store on London's Old Bond Street and, to celebrate the designer's thirty-fourth birthday, will soon launch Kingdom, McQueen's first perfume. In other words, McQueen's brain is a place of hot ideas and his star continues to rise. Liv Tyler wore a simplified version of last season's "Oyster" Dress to the Paris premiere of her movie Lord of the Rings: The Two Towers. *And a bride in New York ordered the full version of the dress at a cost of about 45,000 pounds.*

Inside La Grande Halle de la Villette on the outskirts of Paris, the runway is covered with rocks and ice—an Arctic tundra. A tunnel of Perspex hovers above the catwalk. The soundtrack blares punk icon Sid Vicious singing "My Way." Bathed in red light, Adina Fohlin appears in the tunnel. Slowly, she walks from left to right, West to East, in an A-line skirt and a vest, both trimmed with fur, an outfit for a Siberian princess on a journey.

Styles in this show travel from West to East—over the bleak Siberian tundra, through mountainous Tibet, and on to Japan, Land of the Rising Sun. Dresses and jackets are quilted, some outfits are inspired by fourteenth- and fifteenth-century samurai armor, others by Manga cartoons. There are fur jackets, skirts with pompoms dangling from the hems, and super-tall lace-up boots. Vintage 1950s cuts share the catwalk with bandage dresses and kimono tops.

Left: In her kimono top and red and white headdress, Olivia Inge represents the end of the journey, the East attained.

Above: The skirt panels of Eugenia Volodina's armor-like dress fly out as she walks, affording glimpses of the delicate silk petticoat beneath.

Opposite page: Adina Fohlin in a catsuit and parachute coat fights against the mighty wind.

Below the tunnel, two models quickly crisscross the stage. Natalia Vodianova wears a feathered headdress with a short embroidered jacket, a red top, a quilted green skirt, and high red boots. Leticia Birkheuer marches, arms at her side, in a gold dress. Both models reach the end of the catwalk. They pose side by side, pass by each other, and make way for the next two models.

Adina Fohlin has descended from the walkway. She poses and cedes the space to Erin Wasson in a peaked red hat worn over a military green dress with red trim. Jessica Miller wears a fur jacket covered with metal charms that tinkle as she moves. Daria Werbowy's leather dress is smothered with panels of pink embroidery. The open neck of Karolina Kurkova's black-and-white kimono dress slides off her shoulder as she turns at the end of the catwalk. She tugs the fabric back into place with a deft hand. A couple of leather outfits look as if they could have come straight from the set of the Ridley Scott film *Blade Runner* (1982).

The lights dim, and Adina Fohlin appears once again in the tunnel. Inside, the wind howls. As she struggles forward against the gale, her showpiece parachute coat streams out behind her. The lights come up, and we cross into the East. Laura Morgan struts out in a red and white suit based on the Japanese flag. A number of red and white outfits and a few more fur coats go by, followed by a delicate low-cut dress covered in silver embroidery and worn over red boots. The lights dim again, and the wind tunnel roars to life. A model in underpants fights the wind, her huge ornate kimono blowing out behind her.

Critical reception is mixed. Cathy Horyn of the *New York Times* says: "the special effects overwhelmed the clothes." The *Washington Post*'s Robin Givhan seems horrified by the show's last image. On the other hand, Susannah Frankel of the *Independent* says, "The complexity of the show pieces was juxtaposed with commercial concerns: the balance was just right." And Suzy Menkes of the *International Herald Tribune* writes, "It was a stellar performance."

DELIVERANCE

Spring/Summer 2004

Four months ago, Alexander McQueen was named a Commander of the Order of the British Empire, a great honor. In addition, he was tapped as International Designer of the Year by the Council of Fashion Designers of America. Everyone is eager to see what he's come up with for his new collection. The venue: Salle Wagram, a grand nineteenth-century dance hall in the seventeenth arrondissement of Paris, just steps from the Arc de Triomphe.

McQueen's inspiration for this show comes from *They Shoot Horses, Don't They*, the 1969 Sydney Pollack film starring Jane Fonda and Susannah York. The movie, set during the Great Depression, centers on a group of diverse characters who enter a months-long dance marathon in the hope of winning a cash prize. The grueling dance schedule brings out the worst in the exhausted characters, leading to despondency and even death. As the plot unspools, the inhumanity of the competition becomes increasingly apparent.

Inside the hall: red velvet curtains, crystal chandeliers, a mirrored disco ball, inlaid wood paneling, Greek-style frescos, and a crowd so large that even Kate Moss has to share a seat. The choreography is by Michael Clark, the bad boy of British ballet. Choreography? Once again, McQueen is breaking with catwalk tradition. Lights come up on the dark wood of the sprung dance floor. Seven couples, a mixture of models and professional dancers, each couple in its own spotlight, dance to the sound of big band music. The women are in dresses—a vision of thirties glamour.

In a subversion of the usual catwalk order, McQueen shows his evening wear first. Among the outfits that twirl and tango, Karen Elson wears a floor-length gown of silver sequins that glint with light. The couples on the dance floor hear the same music, and yet each dances in a different style, some moving faster, some slower, giving the proceedings an unsettling, surreal feel.

The big band music segues into a disco song, and the beat picks up. A professional dancer, in the arms of her partner, executes high kicks, raising her leg to the front and back, showing off the full black-feathered skirt of her red-carpet-ready gown. Women in feathered skirts and sleek black satin pants dance by. In the middle of the floor, a professional dancer in a short satin jacket over tiny ruffled pants and crystal-studded thigh-high stockings strikes a pose (page 110). Then, supported by a muscle-bound partner dressed all in white, she executes a standing split, her raised leg pointing straight to the ceiling. Nineteen-year-old Nakiesha, a model recently arrived from Kingston, Jamaica, swings in the arms of her partner. The embroidered sleeves of her semi-sheer dress swirl as she moves.

Opposite page: Michael Clark's choreography allows the dancers to demonstrate their skills while bringing exquisite movement to McQueen's creations.

Right: Nakeisha's bodice of gray jersey with a racerback contrasts with the embroidery and fine material of her dress—a typical McQueen juxtaposition given a new twist.

A dancer in a black mermaid dress twirls in her partner's arms. Another dancer, in a skirt of black feathers with a small Philip Treacy hat firmly attached to her head, flies by on the shoulders of her man. Jessica Miller twirls into the arms of her partner, her long gown sweeping the floor as the big band sound returns. Miller and her partner cast a long, elegant shadow. Under a gray jersey shrug, Lily Cole wears a beautiful dress in delicate peach with long, sheer sleeves that sparkle with crystals and sheer crystal-festooned boots.

The stage is a whirl of motion and color: a very short silver dress with butterfly sleeves, a peach cocktail dress. A dancer's sheer gray dress, embroidered with sequins, sparkles as her partner raises her in a lift. A dramatic burst of orange feathers surrounds another dancer's face. She shimmies, setting the feathers dancing, and turns to reveal the plunging back of her body-hugging gown. On black pants, glittering bands secure the cutout stripe down each side. The dancer within takes center stage with her black-clad, tattooed partner. Dancers circle the stage, each briefly taking the spotlight. Erin Wasson's ensemble seems as if it has been cut from a man's suit and pieced back together with strips of delicate tulle. The lights fade and the music dies as Wasson and her partner leave the stage.

Opposite page: Jessica Miller's bias-cut chiffon gown clings and swings.

Right, top: This elegant low-cut dress recalls McQueen's bumster trousers. McQueen has said that the end of the spine is probably the most erotic spot on the human body.

Right, bottom: Erin Wasson poses in the arms of her dance partner, displaying the tail of her paneled mermaid skirt.

The lights come on again, revealing models and
dancers with toes on a starting line, ready to take off.
As in the Pollack film, the dance-marathon participants
take part in an elimination race. They run around
the room, partners supporting one another, arms
flailing, scarves trailing. The outfits are appropriately
sporty—close-fitting pants with bright racing stripes,
handkerchief-hemmed dresses accented with hot pink.
The pace slows, and the participants pile up, climbing
over one another and sinking to the floor in a heap of
exhaustion. The lights fade.

Dance-marathon participants run around and around the track.
This segment of the show gives the models and dancers
the opportunity to ham it up.

A spotlight picks out Karen Elson on the floor in a beautifully faded floral print dress. To the bluesy sound of "God Bless the Child," written by Billie Holiday and Arthur Herzog, Jr., in 1939, Elson crawls along, staggers to her feet, and almost falls but catches herself with one hand on the floor. Her dance partner joins her and grabs her before she can fall again. They struggle to remain upright, but she slips to her knees, utterly spent. He slides her onto his back and carries her off the stage.

The music gives way to the insistent beat of Portishead's "Strangers" as another model in a delicate print dress is carried about the stage by her partner. A female dancer in a patchwork coat forces herself to kick high—spectacularly high—then as if it has taken all of her energy, she crumples to the floor. Struggling, panting, covered in sweat, their hair disheveled, a few remaining couples force themselves to go on. Gone now are feathers and silks, replaced with denim, patchwork, and plaid. Gone is hope and exuberance. In their place are exhaustion, despondency, despair.

A lone dancer crawls to the center of the stage. She wears a silver sequined gown like Karen Elson's dress from the beginning of the show, but this dress is tarnished and frayed. The dancer sinks to the floor, her chest heaving, and the lights go down. When the lights come back up, the silver-clad dancer remains motionless. The models and dancers trot out, hand in hand, to take a bow. McQueen and Michael Clark run onstage to thunderous applause. They lift the dancer from the floor and together, carry her off.

Audience and critics alike are electrified. Jess Cartner-Morley writes in the *Guardian*: "To put it bluntly, Alexander McQueen's show last night made most other shows on the Paris fashion week schedule look about as dynamic as a Monday morning queue at the Post Office." *The Daily Telegraph*'s Hilary Alexander reports that McQueen "cemented his reputation as the king of spectacle," and Suzy Menkes of the *International Herald Tribune* writes: "McQueen's show, offering both emotion and fine clothes, was at the summit of the summer 2004 season."

PANTHEON AD LECUM

Fall/Winter 2004–05

It is Friday night at the Grande Halle de la Villette. The hall, a converted warehouse space, is dark, as is the round stage. Above the stage loom concentric rings of lights, vibrating with impending action. Spotlights beam down from the outer ring and go out. Music swells: the opening strains of Richard Strauss's Also sprach Zarathustra, *better known as the theme to Stanley Kubrick's* 2001: A Space Odyssey *(1968). A projection: a fiery launch, a rocket powering itself into space. On the catwalk, which resembles a landing pad, a doorway appears. Light pours forth. A silhouette approaches—the first model. She strides forward, following the beams of light. "The show explores the idea of new beginnings," says Alexander McQueen.*

Serge Weinberg, the chief executive of the retail group that owns Alexander McQueen's company, offered McQueen the job as designer at the legendary Yves Saint Laurent. When Weinberg came to London to meet, McQueen did not show. Eventually, McQueen turned down the job. Now, Weinberg and his wife are in the audience. And so are longtime friends Kate Moss and Isabella Blow—wearing one of her signature hats—singer Grace Jones, designer Diane von Furstenberg, and, of course, McQueen's white-haired mother.

Sixteen-year-old Gemma Ward, the first model, takes the stage in a slippery jersey jumpsuit of palest peach. She becomes a just-birthed alien, fresh and exquisitely vulnerable, a creature of light, stepping into a new world. Steven Spielberg's 1977 film *Close Encounters of the Third Kind*, which concerns UFOs and contact with aliens, is said to be an inspiration. And the models look especially otherworldly. Makeup is flat and pale. Hair is gathered into tiny lamb-like curls. Translucent tape pulls at the corners of eyes, elongating them further.

Despite the images of rockets and the theme of aliens from outer space, McQueen has said he wanted this show to be "stripped of all theatrics, so that the focus is purely on design, manufacture, and execution." And the show is subdued, at least for McQueen. One model after another goes by, showing ensembles that are both elegant and wearable. Much of the palette is pale, like Hana Soukupová's exquisitely crafted tweed suit. The pattern on Caroline Trentini's boxy jacket, one of the more colorful garments in this grouping, was inspired by images of crop circles, those mysterious marks found on farmland that some believe are created by the spacecraft of alien beings.

Kate Bush's song "Babooshka," a hit from 1980 that bears her signature otherworldly vocal style, fills the room. Projected images of the surface of the moon, an astronaut in space, solar flares—and the models walk out in evening wear. Viktoria Sekrier and Karen Elson show long dresses ornamented with tribal neckpieces. Katerina and Polina Kouklina model beaded dresses with cutout tops that seem to riff on belly-dance costumes. Then some color creeps into the show: a blue dress, worn by Heather Marks, who also sports large disc earrings by Shaun Leane that cover the sides of her head. A galaxy of stars wheels past, the sun sends out a fiery flare—and the room goes dark.

Opposite page: The fabric of Hana Soukupová's tweed suit glistens with a hint of sparkle from metallic threads worked into the weave.

Above: Variations on the circle theme decorate Caroline Trentini's cropped jacket and slim trousers.

Right: Katerina wears a gown with a cutout beaded top and a filmy patterned skirt.

In the darkness, there is a glowing blue-tinted circle, a blinking light. Like a beacon, the light emanates from a neckpiece worn by Adina Fohlin. She glides majestically around the stage in a stiffened-satin gown that flares out from just below her shoulders to the floor, forming a shape reminiscent of an Apollo command module. Two models join her, one in a dress that glows in the dark, the other with lights flashing from the neckline. The three move around the catwalk solemnly, as if performing a religious rite.

The lights go down again. A harsh beeping, like the cry of a life support system, with an amplified human heartbeat beneath it. Concentric curls of light on the catwalk floor settle into a bull's-eye pattern. Model Tiiu Kuik emerges in a futuristic floor-grazing gown and takes center stage, standing in a bright beam of light. The beeping turns into an ominous steady tone. Face upturned, Kuik raises her arms as if worshipping the pure light. The form of her gown, an exaggerated evening silhouette, is a shock and a revelation. In the *New York Times*, Cathy Horyn sums up the show, writing that McQueen "took the first real step of a designer of his generation to conceive a new line for clothes."

Left: Mateja Penava's glow-in-the-dark dress, which owes much to the geometry of the circle, conceals most of her face.

Opposite page: Tiiu Kuik wears McQueen's extreme version of the classic evening gown with "Orchid" Shoulderpiece, an electroformed silver fantasy by Shaun Leane for Alexander McQueen.

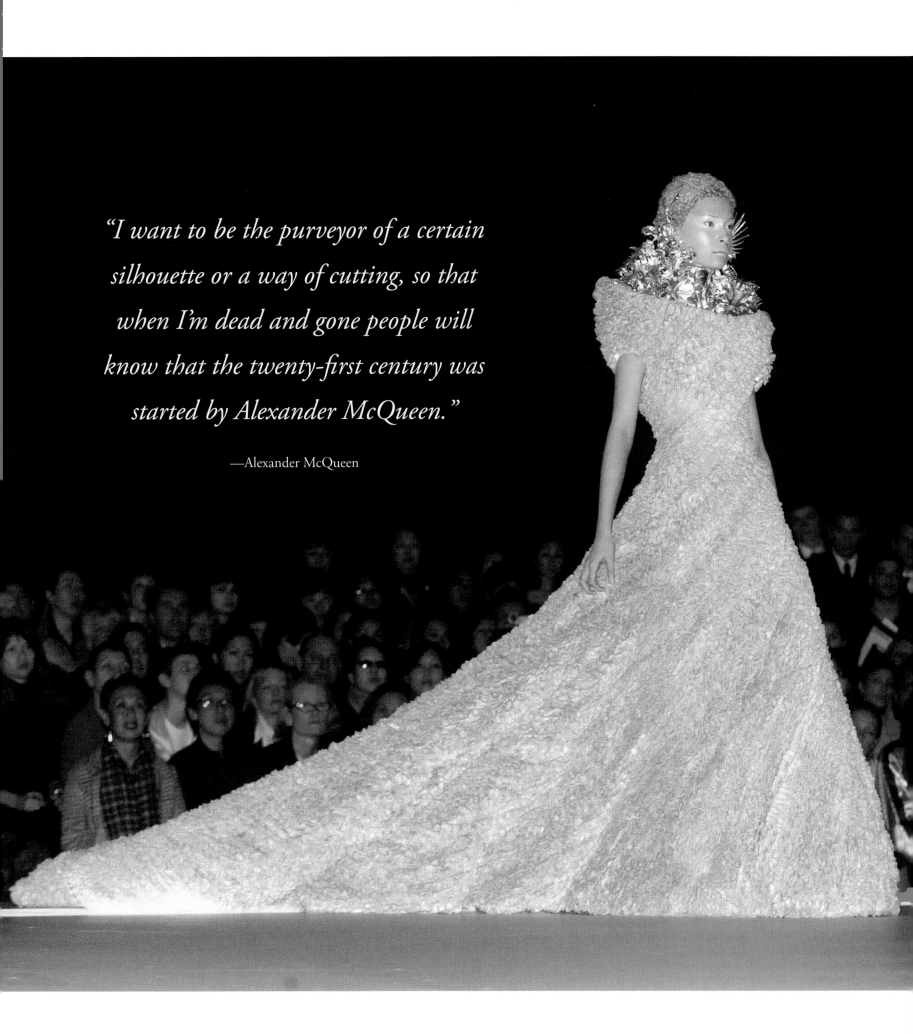

"*I want to be the purveyor of a certain silhouette or a way of cutting, so that when I'm dead and gone people will know that the twenty-first century was started by Alexander McQueen.*"

—Alexander McQueen

IT'S ONLY A GAME

Spring/Summer 2005

The catwalk is a square of bright white, with spectators sitting on

three sides. There is no video screen, and the stage is empty of props.

What could Alexander McQueen be up to this season? By the designer's

standards, his last show was fairly tame. Has he toned down his act? Or

will this be a show of grand pyrotechnics? Two lights flash on, then off

again. A bright spot comes up at the back of the stage. The music bubbles

up with an insistent beat, and the first model strides onto the catwalk.

Once again McQueen has looked to the movies for inspiration, specifically Peter Weir's *Picnic at Hanging Rock* (1975). The film centers on the story of a group of schoolgirls who attend a picnic with two of their teachers on Valentine's Day 1900. Several of the girls and one of the teachers disappear. The period costumes fit right in with McQueen's Edwardian themes. Led by Lily Donaldson in a close-fitting gray school jacket, models wearing riffs on the school uniform march out.

It almost seems like a standard catwalk show. The models cross the stage in a straight line, then travel the perimeter. But then they begin to deviate from the expected. No one leaves the catwalk. Instead, the models form a line, one standing in front of the other, and they remain, motionless, on the stage. One by one, six models, all of whom seem to be Asian, parade out wearing outfits in shades of taupe, including a short skirt embellished with *broderie anglaise*. As the models finish their turns, they form a second line.

The next group of outfits—worn by white models with red hair—are in white and pale green. Then a series of yellow dresses, all on Latina models. Erin Wasson appears in a molded dress of lilac leather with a horsehair skirt. She is followed by lilac and gray ensembles, then Mariacarla Boscano in a similar outfit. Ajuma Nasanyana wears what looks to be a decorative football uniform, complete with helmet and shoulder pads. Gemma Ward appears in a short puffball dress with headgear that resembles an antique Japanese village. The skirt of Hana Soukupová's pink dress matches the shape of Ward's. Natasha Poly wears a bell-shaped appliquéd dress and a leather corset with a high neck.

Left: Katja Shchekina plays the part of a sunny pawn in a cotton dress combining floral prints and broderie anglaise.

Left: As a knight, Mariacarla Boscano wears a molded dress of pale gray leather with a horsehair skirt.

Above: Natasha Poly, a knight for the opposing side, sports a super-high ponytail and a skirt appliquéd with a carousel theme.

Thirty-six models stand on the stage in formation—six rows of six each. The audience begins to applaud. The lights go off. Out of the darkness, an electronic voice announces, "Now we start the game." The lights come up. The floor of the stage glows in a black-and-white checkerboard pattern. The models turn to face one another, forming opposing sides of three rows each. The electronic voice commands "F4 to E3," a chess move, although there seem to be too many pieces. The models in the front row, representing pawns, follow the voice, gliding over the board, changing places, until they have all been eliminated from the game.

The inspiration for McQueen's human chess game was a scene in the 2001 film Harry Potter and the Sorcerer's Stone.

Opposite page: Bishop Shannan Click, in an embroidered lilac silk jacket and obi-style belt, faces off with her opposing bishop, Diana Werbowy, in a diaphanous dress of layered chiffon.

Left: In the game of chess, there are losers and winners. Model Awaoi, in a football helmet decorated in Manga style, plays the winning king.

Daria Werbowy and Shannan Click, as bishops from opposing sides, face off, and Click leaves the board. Gemma Ward and Hana Soukupová, both queens, circle each other, their eyes locked (page 126). Then Soukupová backs down and departs. Ward is then challenged by bishop Werbowy. The queen and the bishop circle around. Finally, Werbowy tosses her head, and Ward leaves the board in defeat. The game continues until checkmate is achieved. The losing king, model Ajuma Nasanyana, drops her head in defeat, her arms hanging limply at her sides. The lights fade. The applause and shouts of "bravo" are deafening. McQueen takes his bow in his standard baggy jeans, which appear to be falling down. Leaving the stage, he hitches them up and breaks into a gallop.

Although Suzy Menkes likes the show, she is not without criticism. Writing in the *International Herald Tribune*, she says: "As an expression of his design spirit, this was one of McQueen's finest shows. Yet he should be enlarging his vocabulary." Susannah Frankel, fashion editor of the *Independent*, writes, "The surprising thing about this particular collection was that it featured so many real clothes. Of course, McQueen wouldn't be McQueen without signature corsetry, exaggeratedly full skirts and fetish footwear. There was a lightness of touch at play here, however, that was positively uplifting."

THE MAN WHO KNEW TOO MUCH

Fall/Winter 2005–06

An iron-railed balcony rings the dark cavernous hall of an old school.

Plaid blankets are handed out to the audience to be draped across their

laps against the chill March air. A row of lights flicks on, bathing the

runway in red. On the balcony, a spotlight flashes, revealing large

arched windows. The light goes out and another comes on, but is

quickly extinguished. Yet again, a spotlight blazes and dies. Suddenly,

a window and doorway are illuminated. A model steps out. A second

door lights up, and a second model appears. They stride along the

balcony, circling the room, and descend the stairs to the catwalk.

This season, Alexander McQueen's show has been inspired by two movies. "The Man Who Knew Too Much," the show's title, references the 1956 Alfred Hitchcock film of the same name. And for a second time, McQueen has looked to *The Birds* (1963), the chilling Hitchcock hit that made Tippi Hedren a star. McQueen loves the precise way that Hitchcock's heroines dressed.

Suits à la Hedren's—slim-fitting skirts, jackets with seven-eighth sleeves—are perfectly tailored, as one would expect from McQueen. In addition, there are sweaters, leather jackets and jeans, cocktail dresses and gowns. In McQueen's imagination, the look and feel of the late fifties and early sixties fuses with Hollywood sizzle to forge something new, a contemporary vision of wearable glamour.

"*For a long time I was looking for my perfect equilibrium, my mojo. And now I think I'm getting there: I've found my customer, my silhouette, my cut. You can hide so much behind theatrics, and I don't need to do that any more.*"

—Alexander McQueen

Left: *Shannan Click carries a green version of McQueen's new "Novak" bag.*

Opposite page: *Julia Stegner sashays down the runway in a mohair sweater and swingy leopard-print skirt.*

Many of the period-style suits, in gray, black, or light taupe, conjure secretaries ready to break out of their mold. The suits are worn with gloves, seamed stockings, and classic pumps. Handbags and shoes match—most of the time. McQueen knows that rules are made to be broken and sends Inguna Butane to the catwalk in a tweed ensemble in shades of tan with black gloves, a black handbag, and acid yellow shoes. The bag, McQueen's "Novak," named after Kim Novak, the star of Hitchcock's *Vertigo* (1958), makes its debut at this show and soon becomes a much sought-after "It" bag, decorating the arms of celebrities and fashionable women alike.

Exotic leopard prints and kittenish mohair knits contrast with the subdued elegance of the suits. Julia Stegner, in a plunging cowl-neck sweater, exemplifies a different mood, a different social sector. Her look calls forth the swanky conviviality of the cocktail lounge.

Outerwear looks range from an impeccably tailored gray tweed coat to sophisticated fur to leather bomber jackets that evoke biker chic. A colorful geometrically patterned poncho embellished with pompoms elicits a cry of "Peru!" from a front-row spectator. The poncho seems to acknowledge the rise of the teenager and that demographic's economic clout. The same could be said for the collection's cropped jeans, patterned sweaters, and multicolored ankle socks.

Tippi Hedren and Kim Novak are not the only stars recalled on this catwalk. Model Hannelore Knuts, a trench coat draped over her shoulders, appears with red lipstick and bleach-blond hair, a perfect Marilyn Monroe. Elise Crombez, too, moves in the Marilyn vein. At the end of the catwalk, she swirls her dress and bends her knees. Arching her back, she gives the photographers a little smile, then turns on her heel and sashays away.

The last pompom- and fringe-adorned model leaves the stage. The lights go down. Is it time for McQueen theatrics? Perhaps one of his signature grand gestures? Spotlights come up on the two staircases and a model appears on each one. Simultaneously, they descend, their long gowns swishing. Halfway down, they pause, posing as they make their grand entrance. On the left, Mariacarla Boscono. On the right, Gemma Ward.

Camera flashes pop throughout the hall. The lights come up as the models sweep onto the runway. Catlike, Boscono slinks, one shoulder dipping with each footfall. Stopping, she slides her hands down her thighs and drops her chin, a movie star from a bygone era. Jessica Stam is a contrast in a vivid red gown with an exaggerated mermaid skirt. A few more evening looks, and the show ends without pyrotechnics. Critics, who have complained that McQueen's work is too dark, angry, and edgy, now accuse him of playing it safe and commercial.

"I used to not care whether people bought the clothes or not, but I kind of like it now. I wouldn't label that commercialism; it's more like I do this work because I want people to wear it."

—Alexander McQueen

Opposite page: *Wearing a lace top and tight-fitting satin skirt under a tailored trench coat, Hannelore Knuts could be the ghost of Marilyn Monroe walking the runway.*

Left: *Jessica Stam takes a turn as a Hollywood starlet in a glamorous floor-sweeping gown.*

NEPTUNE

Spring/Summer 2006

The Imprimerie Nationale is eight kilometers southwest of the center of Paris, two stops from the end of the number 8 metro line. Inside the industrial warehouse, seating is cramped. Journalists have noted that Alexander McQueen often alternates—a quiet, traditional show, then an over-the-top spectacle. Last season's presentation was rather tame; this evening's show is named after the powerful Roman god of water and the sea. So who knows what could happen?

McQueen's inspiration for this show comes from a number of sources: Designers Azzedine Alaïa, who was instrumental in setting the trend of "body-conscious" dressing in the 1980s, and Gianni Versace, whose luxurious clothing walked the line between sexiness and vulgarity and was a feature of that era's power dressing. Grace Jones, another '80s icon is also an inspiration, as is Jean-Paul Goude, the graphic designer and film director who created Jones's look.

The program explains that goddesses and phoenixes are another part of the vision that brought about this collection. As is Guy Bourdin, the influential French fashion photographer, whose work was often narrative and featured violent, sexual, and surrealist imagery. The models are all particularly tall—5 feet 11 inches and over. Makeup is simple and glamorous. Hair is long and slicked back, a wet look— Ursula Andress emerging from the sea in the James Bond movie *Dr. No*.

Left: Mariacarla Boscono's wide embossed belt emphasizes her waist.

Opposite page: The leather harness that McQueen often employs has softened into crystal-adorned straps on Carmen Kass's short sheer dress.

The house lights go down, the music starts, and everything seems to vibrate. At the far end of the enormous room, a light comes on—a pool of white spilling out a doorway. A black clad woman strides forward, and as she moves, the floor in front of her is illuminated, a path of blazing light.

Emina Cunmulaj wears a black suit, black tights, and black patent leather pumps. She marches to the end of the long catwalk and poses with her hands on her hips. Another model wears a beautifully executed suit, rather sensible but for the mini-ness of the skirt. Gemma Ward struts out

in a short black cape, followed by more models in black. Mariacarla Boscono looks fierce in black leather shorts with a wide embossed belt. Her heels seem to dig into the ground like claws.

More black outfits go by, including a pair of leather pants with a tiny midriff-baring jacket. A short dress with a leather harness, shown with silver armbands and gladiator sandals brings to mind Wonder Woman. Carmen Kass walks the runway with lots of snap in a sheer black dress with a little flip at the hem.

Jessica Stam takes a turn in voluminous white, a dangling gold chain at her waist. The music pounds on as the models continue to march forward. Julia Stegner's long-sleeved white gown would look demure if it weren't for a gap from collarbone to waist in the button-down front or the slit starting at the top of the thigh (page 140). Next comes Aleksandra Rastovic in a long white dress with elegantly draped gold chains forming the bodice. A few models carry handbags—the commercial must that McQueen launched last season. There are jewel-encrusted bathing suits, a pantsuit with low button-down lapels, and bandage dresses—very Alaïa, very 1980s.

Hana Soukupová, in a short green dress, makes her return, and the lights go out behind her. As the lights come back up and the models take one last turn, McQueen runs out in jeans and a T-shirt that reads "We love you Kate"—a reference to model Kate Moss who has recently been dropped by several companies for alleged drug use.

Jess Cartner-Morley, fashion editor of the *Guardian*, views McQueen's T-shirt as a deliberate provocation. Others think he is just being a faithful friend. But where *is* the McQueen provocation? What has happened to the bad boy? Sarah Mower of Style.com is disappointed: "Though some of his moves are clearly being made in an effort to sell—no criticism in itself—this show, from a designer whose capabilities have won such respect, was a letdown."

Opposite page: Doutzen Kroes carries a Novak bag. This season they come in sepia snakeskin, leather with gold studs, ostrich, and patent snakeskin.

Right, top: The sheer embroidered panel in the back of Jessica Stam's gown exposes her entire back as well as her bum cleavage.

Right, bottom: Alexander McQueen wears a T-shirt proclaiming his support for shunned model Kate Moss.

WIDOWS OF CULLODEN

Fall/Winter 2006–07

The invitation bears the mysterious words Bantraich de cuil Lodair, *Scottish Gaelic for "Widows of Culloden." The event is held about two miles from the center of Paris, south of the Gare de Lyon, an area not well known to foreign visitors. The show has tough security, and once inside, the mysteries continue. Rough wooden boards cover the catwalk. A glass pyramid rises from the center, and the surrounding benches are covered in hemp. Stickers at each seat proclaim that the show is dedicated to Alexander McQueen's friend and early patron, Isabella Blow.*

As many as two thousand Scotsmen died in the Battle of Culloden, the last battle of the Jacobite Rising of the 1740s. The Jacobites, who supported the return of a Stuart to the throne of Great Britain and were led by Charles Edward Stuart, known as Bonnie Prince Charlie, lost the battle to the royal forces of George II. After Culloden, government troops brutally suppressed the Highland clans. The chiefs were stripped of their weapons and legal authority. Estates were seized. The wearing of kilts and tartan, the symbols of the clans, was banned. In "Widows of Culloden," McQueen memorializes the strong Scotland that was and the warrior spirit that still lives.

The fifty ensembles in the collection are almost a reprise of McQueen's greatest hits—smart tailoring, tweed, nipped-in waists, padded hips, bustles, torn chiffon, lace, the confrontation of fragility and strength, a dark Romanticism—but it is the old made new again. Susannah Frankel, fashion editor of the *Independent*, sees this show as McQueen's "return to the unbridled spectacle and raw power with which he made his name." The clothes, of course, are spectacular, but it will be the moment of surprise sparked by McQueen's showmanship at the end that becomes the iconic image of the show, the image that lives on in hearts and minds.

Snejana Onopka, the first model to appear on the rough-hewn boards, wears a tweed suit and a headpiece crafted by Shaun Leane and Philip Treacy. Jeweler Leane created the silver, gem-encrusted eggs and wove the nest by hand. McQueen wanted the eggs to be speckled, like duck eggs, so Leane used a mix of blue and brown stones. Treacy then attached mallard wings to complete the look. Leane sees the nest and eggs as symbolic of new beginnings.

Feathers and bird wings lend the models a mythic quality, elevating them above the earthbound human. The use of tartan, of course, harks back to McQueen's controversial 1995 show "Highland Rape," which also references the subjugation of Scotland. Here, the tartan is more polished, softened with ruffles and embroidery, and the models, who strut to the music of bagpipes with a heavy punk beat, are not victims. They carry the attitude of warrior princesses.

"I wanted to start from the crux, and the crux is my heritage."

—Alexander McQueen

Left: *Marta Berzkalna in a jumpsuit of McQueen tartan, a ruffled black cotton shirt with* broderie anglaise, *and a headpiece of pheasant tail feathers*

Opposite page: *Snejana Onopka's headpiece, by Shaun Leane and Philip Treacy for Alexander McQueen, features silver, Swarovski gemstones (blue topaz, smoky quartz), and mallard wings.*

148

After the tartans and some slinky black-velvet evening wear, Raquel Zimmermann appears dressed from head to toe in cream-colored lace, a fairy-tale bride. Or, perhaps, an otherworldly one, as she sports white antlers. Is this beautiful horned creature trapped in the lace and trying to get out? Or is the lace her protection, a magical filigreed armor that will keep her from harm?

Zimmerman's ruffled lace dress was inspired by the handcrafted gown that designer Sarah Burton wore at her own wedding. Burton describes the fabrication: "We cut out all of the flowers from the lace and reappliquéd them on tulle to make our own fabric." Burton calls the technique a marriage of traditional textiles and lace with modern structure and design. The making of the old into something new is a theme that runs throughout McQueen's work.

Nature is also important in McQueen's work, and it is nature made new. Antlers crafted of Perspex, a kind of acrylic, by Philip Treacy, tie the natural world to the world of artifice. Feathers as headdresses, an entire gown constructed from pheasant plumes, swaths of lacy ruffles so densely layered that they recall a bird's coat all lend weightlessness, glamour, and even majesty to the women on the runway.

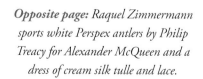

Opposite page: Raquel Zimmermann sports white Perspex antlers by Philip Treacy for Alexander McQueen and a dress of cream silk tulle and lace.

Right: White embroidery and a cutout in the top of Lily Donaldson's black-velvet gown accentuate her curves.

"I get my
ideas out of my
dreams . . . if you're
lucky enough to use
something you see
in a dream, it is
purely original. It's
not in the world—
it's in your head."

—Alexander McQueen

Gemma Ward in a lavishly ruffled white dress is followed by three more evening looks, including a gorgeous off-the-shoulder gown with a voluminous pouf skirt worn by Hana Soukupová. The most spectacular moment, however, is still to come.

The final model exits the catwalk, the lights dim, and a glow appears inside the pyramid. The glowing shape swirls, as if unfolding, and a vague form begins to appear—a woman, a woman in a chiffon dress that undulates around her (page 146). Slowly, she grows clearer and more defined. She is Kate Moss, the supermodel missing from the runway since her 2005 drug scandal. The holographic image of Moss dances in her dress. Moss is absent and yet she is present—a spectacle, a specter, a ghost, like the dead Scottish warriors of Culloden and like the widows who survived them. The crowd cheers and gives McQueen a standing ovation. "The hologram of Moss," writes Lorraine Candy, editor-in-chief of *Elle* magazine, "was all we talked about for months afterwards."

Left: Hana Soukupová's gown is made feminine not by ruffles but by swaths of softly gathered material and the raised hemline of her long bubble skirt.

Opposite page: Gemma Ward, adorned with butterflies, wears a ruffled gown of ivory silk organza.

SARABANDE

Spring/Summer 2007

The Cirque d'Hiver, opened by Emperor Napoleon III in 1852 on the Right Bank in Paris, holds a special place in fashion history. This is where Richard Avedon took his iconic photo Dovima with Elephants. *And this is the venue Alexander McQueen has chosen to showcase his new collection. The audience files in and takes seats around the circular stage. In the center, a chandelier flashing with light hovers just above the floor. A harpsichord begins to play, and the chandelier slowly rises, casting ghostly shadows and illuminating a chamber orchestra. The violins join the stately tune, and the first model walks out.*

The orchestra plays Sarabande, the fourth movement of the Keyboard Suite in D Minor, by George Frideric Handel. McQueen found inspiration in the composition and in the 1975 Stanley Kubrick film *Barry Lyndon*, which features this musical theme. Other sources of inspiration include the paintings of Francisco de Goya and the eccentric socialite and fashion icon Marchesa Luisa Casati. Muse and patron to a number of artists and writers, Casati was well known for declaring, "I want to be a living work of art."

The mood is romantic, nostalgic, even elegiac. The chandelier, draped with bits of torn chiffon, appears dusty and festooned with cobwebs. The models look ghostly, with white makeup on their faces and ears, and streaked down their necks. Their hair is worn up, but often seems to be falling down. The collection harks back to the turn-of-the-century Edwardian era, the last hurrah of the traditional aristocracy. Riding jackets and skirts appear, menswear-inspired suits, infanta dresses, corseted shapes, and finally, real flowers—lots of flowers.

Daiane Conterato, the first model, crosses the stage, then loops around the musicians who sit in two groups on opposite sides of the circle. Walking her figure eight, she looks as if she has stepped from a portrait by John Singer Sargent, who was renowned for his paintings of upper-class Edwardian women. While Conterato's frock coat is period menswear, its asymmetrical closure lends softness as does her ruffled blouse. Much of this collection is black and white, a study in contrasts. McQueen often plays with such dynamic tensions— masculine versus feminine, hard verus soft, dead versus alive.

The monobosom, or pigeon-breasted, corset in the Edwardian era was designed to conceal the natural shape of the breasts. Snejana Onopka's pony-skin corset seems to defy that history in its celebration of the female form (page 154). While the corset serves as a kind of armor, her soft, off-the-shoulder ruffled shirt gives the outfit a louche sense of ease. In contrast to Onopka's dishabille, Vlada Roslyakova looks smart and ready for the races in a bowler, cutaway jacket, and high-waisted skirt. Gamine and boyish in a pantsuit with a short beaded jacket, Irina Lazareanu prances across the stage.

Left: Irina Lazareanu's outfit is enlivened with beads and headgear by Philip Treacy.

Opposite page: Vlada Roslyakova's equestrian-inspired skirt is paired with a hat and jacket from menswear. The bird print of her skirt is echoed by a single bird on the back left shoulder of her jacket.

Black dresses with padded hips go by, a few more suits, a gray dress and suit with overlays of black netting. All gorgeous, all perfectly tailored. The music speeds up. The arms of the string players, all clad in gray, seem to fly over their instruments. A few audience members fan themselves with their programs. Anna Baruskova appears, a ghostly bride, her face covered with a smoky gray veil sparkling with lilac crystals. Underneath, she wears a crown of flowers. Her strapless dress is generously padded at the hips, creating exaggerated womanly curves.

Freja Beha Erichsen, her face a deathly pale, models a black dress with a skirt completely covered in feathers, and there are sheer gowns of lace—sexy yet restrained—and another bird print appears, this time on a floor-grazing white dress. Kim Noorda wears a gray pinstripe suit like every Edwardian gentleman owned, but with a new twist. The lapels of this suit have grown into sashes that cross over the chest and tie behind. Instead of wool, the back of the jacket offers a surprise—shiny, silver-colored satin.

Left: *Her features obscured by embroidery, Anna Barsukova looks particularly ghostly. The padding at the sides of her infanta dress emphasizes the hips and the hourglass female form.*

Opposite page: *Mimi Roche looks ethereal in her long dress with its sheer skirt and translucent top embroidered with flowers.*

The blacks, whites, and grays from earlier in the show give way to colors, muted colors: lilac, mauve, light pink, dusty pink—what the Edwardians called "ashes of roses." Raquel Zimmermann emerges from the darkness. Her structured silk dress contains flowers, both real and artificial. Flowers pour from her sleeves and neckline, and it is flowers that pad her hips.

As if all this beauty, all this spectacle, weren't enough, one more model takes the stage. Tanya Dziahileva is clad entirely in real flowers, a sweeping gown of blooms with a high Edwardian neck and structured shoulders. Her image conjures visions of pre-Raphaelite paintings and of the French stage and early film actress Sarah Bernhard, who was photographed in a coffin where she was said to sleep. The model reaches the center of the stage and continues, veering to the right to make her first loop. Flowers fall from her dress to the floor. The audience applauds as she continues at a measured, stately pace, trailing blossoms as she goes.

Right: In an interview, Raquel Zimmermann says she feels great wearing such a dress and that the flowers smell wonderful.

Opposite page: The frozen flowers on Tanya Dziahileva's gown begin to thaw and fall to the floor as she walks the runway.

> *"Things rot. It was all about decay. I used flowers because they die."*
>
> —Alexander McQueen

The applause continues. The lights go down and come up again. The orchestra plays an instrumental version of the Rolling Stones song "Paint It, Black" as the models parade around the stage. McQueen appears in the doorway wearing jeans and sneakers. Shyly, he waves, then disappears backstage. The crowd cheers.

After the superb theatricality of McQueen's "Widows of Culloden" show, critics had imagined that "Sarabande" would be less grand. But McQueen has done it again. "We were given this gift tonight," says *Vanity Fair* editor Elizabeth Saltzman Walker. And Alexandra Shulman of British *Vogue* says of McQueen, "He has this great sense of drama—always."

IN MEMORY OF ELIZABETH HOW

Fall/Winter 2007–08

It's a rainy Friday night. Traffic is terrible, and the venue of Alexander McQueen's new show is distant—more than six kilometers from the center of Paris. Damp audience members hurry inside the Zénith de Paris, one of the city's largest halls, site of rock concerts and World Wrestling Entertainment events. On each seat lies a black envelope. Inside is a genealogy chart tracing McQueen's roots back to Elizabeth How, who was hanged during the Salem witch trials. On the floor of the stage glows a large red pentagram. Above the stage, three enormous female faces peer down from a screen shaped like an inverted pyramid. Wind lifts wisps of their hair. Shadows flicker across their faces. The sounds of urgent whispering fill the room. A scream. A bright flash and the image goes dark. The rising sun fills the screen. The rapid beat of Agent Provocateur's "Red Tape" fires up, and the first model materializes, stepping out into the dawn's glow.

Like "Widows of Culloden" (fall/winter 2006–07), this show was inspired by McQueen's heritage. His ancestor Elizabeth How was hanged as a witch on July 19, 1692. By all accounts, How was a strong woman. She was married to a blind farmer and thus took on some of the tasks that were reserved for men at the time. Accordingly, her community viewed her as not properly submissive.

Many victims of Salem's notorious purge were outsiders, those who did not conform in looks, behavior, or beliefs to the narrow idea of women's proper role. Themes of persecution and the stigmatization of the "other" crop up in McQueen's work again and again. Here, he explores witchcraft through paganism, Ancient Egypt, and the worship of the sun and the moon.

"*If you have half an hour of someone's attention, then you have got to make it half an hour that they remember for the rest of their lives.*"

—Alexander McQueen

Left: Magdalena Frackowiak wears a blue and gold cocktail dress with origami-like points, which perhaps echo the points of the pentagram onstage. They also recall a 1989 design by Issey Miyake.

Opposite page: In her glittering gold suit, Caroline Trentini glows like the sun, an object of worship for many pagan cults and some Ancient Egyptians.

A spotlight follows Catherine McNeil as she walks along a line of the red pentagram on the darkened stage. Both the front and back of her pod-like dress bulge outward, quite a departure from the exaggerated hourglass figure of last season's "Sarabande." When McNeil reaches one of the pentagram's points, she turns on her heel and moving widdershins—that's witch-speak for counterclockwise—she traces another line of the red figure.

A swarm of writhing locusts appears on the screen as the models crisscross the pentagram, their hair jutting out behind their heads in elongated buns. Both hair and makeup are inspired by Ancient Egypt via Elizabeth Taylor's look in the 1963 film *Cleopatra*. The blue and gold pattern of Magdalena Frackowiak's smashing cocktail dress looks as if it were lifted from the painted coffin of an Egyptian queen. Snejana Onopka, all in gold, resembles a statue of a forgotten and once-powerful goddess.

The music switches to drumming, and the immense face of an owl materializes on the screen (page 162). Caroline Trentini strides out in a catsuit covered in gold paillettes—except for the smooth gold breastplate molded to the shape of her upper torso. Over the sound system blasts a hard rock version of "I Put a Spell on You." Once again, the huge faces of women hover overhead. Below, a stiff, shaped bodice extends down over the hips and up over a model's face, leaving only her heavily made-up eyes visible.

On the screen, a giant grinning skull morphs into a bloodied face and bursts into flames. Mariya Markina takes the stage in a short green satin parka. Dolly Jones, the editor of Britain's Vogue.com, predicts that this jacket will be McQueen's next commercial hit. Electric guitars wail as Egle Tvirbutaite models a short black dress backed by a molded panel of gold, which gleams brightly in the darkness. Overhead, the image of a woman's face flickers and changes into a skull that, in turn, dissolves into flame.

Vlada Roslyakova's outfit contrasts hard and soft with an outer layer that's stiff and an inner one that appears almost fluffy. The wide neckline recalls one of the amazing futuristic dresses from McQueen's "Pantheon ad Lecum" collection (fall/winter 2004–05). The flames on the screen burn out, and the rising moon appears as more black outfits go by, including another commercially viable parka, this one with a nipped-in waist. Above, hands alternate with giant faces that seem to drip with blood.

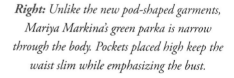

Right: *Unlike the new pod-shaped garments, Mariya Markina's green parka is narrow through the body. Pockets placed high keep the waist slim while emphasizing the bust.*

Opposite page: *The exaggerated hourglass silhouette of Vlada Roslyakova's ensemble is a typical Alexander McQueen shape. The juxtaposition of hard and soft—strength and vulnerability—is also found frequently in the designer's work.*

On the overhead screen dangles a woman's naked body, her arms upraised and her hands clutching a man's bare shoulders. Below, a parade of models in evening wear takes the stage. Kinga Rajzak is bewitching as she rounds the pentagram in a billow of green and black silk. Eva Poloniova also sports green and black, and her long dress, which trails on the floor, is slit to the hip. Anna Barsukova, in a semi-sheer gown and a moon headdress, looks serene, a goddess-like point of stillness. A shiny floor-length mermaid dress, beaded body suits, and gowns of sheer black netting, one with a matching mask that chills the heart, and the spectacle is over. Above, a blurry face, then the words "Elizabeth How, 1692" appear.

The critics are not pleased. Soothed by the gentle beauty of the previous season's "Sarabande," they had not anticipated this show with its macabre and distracting theatrics. They seem to have forgotten the angry, confrontational McQueen of earlier collections. Suzy Menkes of the *International Herald Tribune* says, "Another great showman tried hard, too hard to turn fashion into theater," and Style.com's Sarah Mower says that the show is "one of the season's most deleterious cases of concept overwhelming clothes."

Right: The tilted, gem-encrusted cross embroidered on Kinga Rajzak's green and black dress recalls the ecclesiastic look of McQueen's "Irere" collection (spring/summer 2003).

Left: As Olga Sherer walks the pentagram, the gold embroidery on her velvet gown looks like the flickering of flames in the night.

Above: Anna Barsukova could be worshipped as a moon goddess. Her headdress of silver and moonstones is by Shaun Leane for Alexander McQueen.

LA DAME BLEUE

Spring/Summer 2008

The invitation comes with a poster, a full-color illustration of Isabella Blow in a chariot drawn by a pair of winged horses. She wears an Alexander McQueen dress, Philip Treacy headgear, and an enormous pair of white wings. Blow, McQueen's patron and muse, has died—and by her own hand. The show is a tribute to her, a sartorial memorial.

Ever since Blow saw McQueen's graduate show, tracked him down, and purchased the collection, she championed his work and wore his clothes—on the street and in the pages of magazines. Although she was not wealthy, she acted as his patron as well as his muse and confidant. McQueen lived on a floor of Blow's London house for a time and spent weekends with her and her husband at Hilles, their country house in Gloucestershire. It was Blow who accompanied McQueen to Paris to sign his contract with Givenchy in 1996. Many expected him to hire her as a stylist when he went to the venerable house, but that was not to be.

Compared to the distant venue of McQueen's last show, the Palais Omnisports de Paris-Bercy seems close to the center of Paris. Viewed from the reflecting pool, the arena resembles an enormous winged figure. Could that be why McQueen chose the site for his homage to Blow? Inside, the air smells of Fracas, Blow's signature scent created by the French couturier Robert Piguet. A bottle of the perfume nestles inside the small round pink and black box on each seat. A flapping sound is heard and at one end of the catwalk, a huge light installation begins to flash, simulating the movement of wings, an enormous bird accelerating into flight. An avian screech, the beat of a disco song, and the show begins.

The glossy surface of the catwalk reflects the wings of light, duplicating their pulsating pattern. Alice Gibb walks from between the wings and straight to the end of the catwalk and back again. She wears a suit with a cropped jacket, padded shoulders, and short sleeves with a Philip Treacy hat. Next out is Snejana Onopka in a traditional menswear fabric, Prince of Wales check. Her jacket has strong shoulders and sharp, exaggerated hips, while the pleated skirt has a softer, more feminine feel, a very smart outfit to wear to the office.

Alana Zimmer's neutral dress and wide obi-style belt are also office ready. Her butterfly headdress—another Philip Treacy stunner—is made from turkey feathers that have been painted and shaped by hand. Treacy was another of Isabella Blow's protégés. He, too, once lived on a floor of her house, and she was often seen wearing his fantastic creations.

"Isabella flew. The collection is exuberant and excessive. It's about her way of thinking and that way of thinking brought light into fashion."

—Alexander McQueen

Opposite page: *With her suit, Alice Gibb wears a hat of silk netting decorated with a Swarovski crystal dragonfly by Philip Treacy for Alexander McQueen.*

Left: *Alana Zimmer's headwear would have delighted Isabella Blow, who often wore hats that dipped in front of her eyes or covered her face.*

Not for the shy, Chanel Iman's trapezoidal dress seems to reference the Japanese designers Isabella Blow also admired. Black-and-white feathers glued directly to the model's shoulders add to the avian theme. Blow was fond of birds, as is McQueen. Once she even arranged for two falconers to visit her country house so that McQueen could learn about their birds.

Next come light-as-air cinched-waist chiffon dresses in white and pink, dresses covered entirely in feathers, and kimono-style looks with strong defined shoulders. Sheila Marquez's black dress—which seems like this season's wide belt gone wild, expanding to cover the entire body—recalls a bird cage or a particularly delicate suit of armor.

Left: The cage-like creation on Sheila Marquez seems to both protect and reveal. The dress lends strength, while highlighting the wearer's fragility.

Above: The geometric construction of Chanel Iman's dress seems hard, but the garment and the model seem to float with a certain kind of romance.

The light installation shimmers purple and white, then goes fuchsia. For a split second, the lights go out. On again, they emit a red glow before returning to a pulsating purple and white. A model in a suit with tiny shorts goes by, followed by others in a skirt suit, a black evening dress with gold wings protectively folded around the shoulders, and a short dress of white and gold brocade. Vlada Roslyakova's form-fitting pink dress, a re-creation of a McQueen design from Givenchy, is a style that Blow owned. Blow loved this McQueen silhouette—strong shoulders and a tiny waist. McQueen created each outfit in the show on the actual model for a precise, curve-revealing fit.

Right: Vlada Roslyakova's fitted pink python dress shimmers in the lights of the catwalk.

A pink and black dress, glittering wings at the shoulders, floats by, then Daul Kim appears, simple and elegant in black with pink highlights. Daiane Conterato wears super-high chopine sandals and a huge Philip Treacy headdress with a floral motif. A number of rainbow-colored dresses, printed to look like feathers and reminiscent of McQueen's "Irere" collection (spring/summer 2003), sail by. The bodice of Natasha Poly's black floor-length gown is embellished with bird wings, which continue under the arm and wrap around her body—protective avian armor.

Tasked with surrounding the model with light, Shaun Leane created a gleaming silver visor of fifteen narrow parallel bars that sprout up and back from Alice Gibb's waist then bend twice to cross over her shoulders and in front of her face. Raquel Zimmerman, the last model to walk, seems ready to soar in a full-length gown completely covered with feathers. The room gets darker and the light installation glows red as Zimmerman retreats and finally disappears beneath the giant wings.

The applause begins as the models parade out to Neil Diamond's "Play Me" (page 170). McQueen and Treacy step out to more applause. Many in the audience are in tears, mourning Blow, a true talent and one of fashion's great nurturers. The critics love the show and the collection, and they seem to appreciate the relatively low-key presentation. As Dolly Jones of British *Vogue* writes, "Reigning in [McQueen's] penchant for showmanship—though gigantic feathered collars ensured it was still very much evident—meant his talent was, in fact, all the more obvious and it was refreshing to just sit back, for once, and enjoy the clothes."

Opposite page: Parrot feathers burst from the top of Viviane Orth's colorful diaphanous dress.

Above: Raquel Zimmermann takes on the beauty and power of a bird in this sweeping feather-covered gown and a dramatic headdress suggestive of the wings worn by Isabella Blow in the show's poster.

THE GIRL WHO LIVED IN THE TREE

Fall/Winter 2008–09

The invitation, etched on gold-tone paper, bears an image of a tree and on the next page, the image of a girl, whose long sinuous hair blends with the tree branches. Once again, the Alexander McQueen show takes place at the Palais Omnisports de Paris-Bercy. In the center of the stage towers a huge tree wrapped in silk tulle. The fabric fans out, completely covering the square stage. "I've got a 600-year-old elm tree in my garden," McQueen explains, "and I made up this story of a girl who lives in it and comes out of the darkness to meet a prince and become a queen."

McQueen has recently spent a month traveling in India with his friend and frequent collaborator Shaun Leane. The influence of this trip can be seen in the sari silks, rich embroidery, jewel-encrusted headdresses, and flat slippers of this collection. And something new can be felt: a sense of serenity and calm. Other sources of inspiration include the queens of England, toy soldiers, and the Duke of Wellington.

The girl who lives in McQueen's tree starts out as a punk princess. She's rather dark and a bit of a ragamuffin with wild frizzy hair and a defined brow. At the same time, she's romantic. She could be the little sister of Edward Scissorhands, brought to life by Johnny Depp in Tim Burton's 1990 film of the same name. To an orchestral version of Nirvana's "Come as You Are," she steps onto the catwalk, circles the magical tree, and the fairy tale begins.

Amanda Laine is the first model to embody McQueen's feral, arboreal heroine. Although her black asymmetrical crinoline dress seems made for dancing, she walks at a measured pace. Kasia Struss's black outfit is more masculine. Impeccably tailored—as always with McQueen—the suit's hardness and linearity are softened by the pattern embossed into the material and by the bows at the neckline and wrists of her blouse.

Iris Strubegger walks carefully, balancing what appears to be a skeletal peacock on her head. On further inspection, her headdress proves to be coral and twigs, expertly crafted by Philip Treacy, melding McQueen's bird theme with the tree of the show. The volume of Strubegger's leg-of-mutton sleeves and bubble skirt accentuate the slimness of her waist.

Above: Kasia Struss stops to pose in a pantsuit that fits like the proverbial glove.

Right: Here, two peacocks—crafted from cutout black lace—spread their splendid tails to wrap around Georgina Stojikovic's ivory silk skirt, an avian embrace.

With Georgina Stojilkovic, our punk princess has come down from her tree. In her ivory tulle dress she seems brighter and tamer. She looks at the audience askance, very bird-like. Her ruffled petticoats—light as feathers—move with her and add to her avian air. The pair of peacocks at her breast suggests courtship and romance. The peacock, the national bird of India, is associated with beauty, grace, and love. Is the princess ready to meet her mate? Is she ready to fall in love? The lights fade. The tree glows blue. For a moment, the stage is empty. Slowly, the lights come up again, the yellow of dawn. In this new day, a transformation is about to take place.

Left: Iris Strubegger's avian crown, by Philip Treacy for Alexander McQueen, is both lovely and macabre, perfect for a punk princess.

The fabric stretched across the stage seems to glow in the light. Natasha Poly steps out, a fairytale vision in red and white. Our punk heroine has shed her darkness. Makeup is lighter, hair more soigné but still a bit unorthodox. Instead of sitting at the nape of the neck, the chignon is at the top of the head, with a crown-like fan of hair that retains a certain punk attitude. And then there are the jewels: elaborate gem-encrusted headpieces, antique necklaces, and opulent earrings so long they graze the shoulder—millions of dollars worth of rubies, diamonds, and other precious stones set with exquisite craftsmanship—all from Jaipur's Gem Palace, run by the Kasliwals, who were once court jewelers to Mughal emperors.

Right: Taryn Davidson's red silk dress with silver jacquard borders does seem fit for a princess.

182

The ensembles owe much to the wardrobe of the young Queen Elizabeth II and her dressmakers Norman Hartnell, who made her 1953 coronation gown, and Hardy Amies, both a tailor and a dressmaker as well as the creator of costumes for Stanley Kubrick's *2001: A Space Odyssey* (1968). Taryn Davidson's dress, however, is inspired by India— a sari silk in jewel tones worn over a long ivory petticoat. Magdalena Frackowiak, surrounded by airy ruffles, is no less exotic. Her bolero jacket is silk velvet embellished with gold. Raquel Zimmermann looks androgynous in long high-waisted pants and a cropped jacket. In an interview, she explains that she plays the role of the prince, and a noble prince she is. The print of Siri Tolerød's crinoline dress—images of Queen Elizabeth tilted sideways— gives a hint that McQueen, for all his romanticism, for all his apparent glorification of the British Empire, is still a rebel at heart.

Right: Magdalena Frackowiak's *ivory tulle dress is knotted at the hem, which gives her noble attitude a casual punky spin.*

Rich blue velvets, one elaborately stitched with gold, an ermine coat, "New Look" silhouettes, feathered creations—one yellow, one red—and a nearly translucent ivory Empire dress pass by, all worn by models with white tights and flat, embroidered slippers. Then comes Tanya Dziahileva, who couldn't look more royal in her red silk bolero jacket and bejeweled silk tulle dress, followed by Snejana Onopka, a vision in gold. And, finally, out steps Alyona Osmanova. In a bejeweled ivory silk gown and red satin coat that sweeps the floor, she is regal, she is resplendent, she is a queen. Our punk princess has made the journey down from her tree and been transformed. As our new queen takes her stately walk around the stage, the audience begins to applaud.

For the most part, critics and audience alike feel this show to be a triumph. In her review on Style.com, Sarah Mower writes of McQueen, "It was a day when his brilliance had never shone more brightly." Suzy Menkes, fashion editor at the *International Herald Tribune* remarks on the beauty of the short crinoline dresses, but unlike Mower, who thought there was "plenty to wear" in the collection, Menkes complains "that there was little to wear." Summing up the feelings of many, Dolly Jones of British *Vogue* writes: "More than 1,000 of us sat spellbound as one of the most beautiful fashion fairy tales of our age was unveiled."

Left: Tanya Dziahileva's ivory dress of silk tulle is embellished with red glass crystals.

Opposite page: *Alyona Osmanova, as the queen, wears a billowy satin coat and a gown of ivory silk chiffon. Her matching bag recalls the fantasy of a Fabergé egg.*

NATURAL DIS-TINCTION
UN-NATURAL SELECTION

Spring/Summer 2009

A headshot of Alexander McQueen that morphs into the image of a skull: this is the lenticular print on the invitation. The Paris venue, Le 104, an art space in the nineteenth arrondissement, was once a city morgue. Could this be McQueen's perfect space? He is on a roll. Last season, in addition to showing a critically acclaimed collection, his company announced a profit for the first time. And a flagship McQueen boutique has opened in Los Angeles. All of this means that McQueen's skull-imprinted invite is one hot, hot ticket.

Inside Le 104, the hall is cavernous. Overhead, the large glass skylight is full of darkness. At one end of the room is a veritable zoo of taxidermy animals: elephant, giraffe, hippopotamus, leopard, llama, polar bear, rhinoceros, tiger, zebra. Program notes explain that the collection is inspired by Charles Darwin's *On the Origin of Species* (1859). McQueen has been thinking about evolution, Earth's raw materials, the Industrial Revolution and its effects, and looking at concepts of nature versus technology.

The riches of Earth—wood, crystals, flowers—appear in engineered prints, fabric printed specifically for each piece of a garment rather than being cut from an all-over graphic design. In other words, the sleeves have their own print, as does the bodice and the collar. McQueen also references the Eiffel Tower, diamonds, and, of course, a McQueen favorite—skeletons. Finally, the audience is seated. The lights go down. On a screen above and behind the animals appears an image of our mother ship, the revolving Earth.

Over the loudspeakers comes the sound of a stampede—a roar, hoofbeats, and the trumpeting of elephants. A misty light rises between the stuffed animals. The light grows in intensity, and the animal sounds get louder. A silhouette appears in the mist, and Sigrid Agren moves forward in a wood-grain print. The silk fabric of Kelli Lumi's frock coat and skinny trousers, also in a wood-grain print, lends her outfit exceptional lightness and fluidity as she walks to a perky electronic dance beat.

Lily Donaldson, in her shift with pink flowers trapped beneath, appears like a fairy in bloom. Like all the models, she wears a hairnet over her face with vein-like strands of hair captured beneath, heightening her otherworldly air. The corset and exaggerated hips of Diana Farkhullina's outfit are typical McQueen, as are the high Edwardian collar and leg-of-mutton sleeves. The fabric features a botanical print with butterflies and other insects among the flowers.

Opposite page: The strong silhouette of Diana Farkhullina's dress is pure McQueen.

Below, left: The flowers of Lily Donaldson's dress are caught and seemingly pressed between layers of fabric like the botanical specimens that Darwin collected.

Below, right: The delicate billowing fabric of Anna Jagodzinska's white dress is offset by a signature McQueen skull—perhaps a reminder of what lies underneath all beauty.

Chanel Iman's sexy flapper dress is a far cry from buttoned-up Edwardiana. Her barely there frock, in pink and gray, features looped silk fringe that sways as she struts the catwalk, producing a fluid movement that reminds one critic of birds in flight. Layers of looped fringe in a shiny gray dégradé cover the bodice and make up the mobile skirt of Alyona Osmanova's flirty dress. Embroidery starts at the shoulder and carries over to the back, where McQueen's bird and botanical theme enhance the model's almost-bare skin.

With her strong-shouldered coat and jewel-like second skin, Magdelena Frackowiak could be a visiting dignitary from another planet. If the earlier dresses represented the natural world, this shimmering bodysuit and long jacket are all about technology and the future. So, too, are the look-alike three-dimensional flowers that cover Karlie Kloss's yellow minidress. Its stiffened bodice is topped by sheer fabric embroidered with more flowers that continue down the sleeves.

Opposite page, left: Chanel Imam's dress of looped fringe is all about sensual movement.

Opposite page, right: The stiff bell-shaped skirt of Karlie Kloss's minidress gently sways as she sashays along the catwalk.

Right: Magdalena Frackowiak looks like an alien being in her bejeweled bodysuit.

Two more flower-covered minidresses are followed by ensembles in colorful kaleidoscopic crystal prints and black-and-white crystal patterns that appear to morph into skeletons, perhaps in anticipation of a future melding of human and machine. The crystal/skeleton print worn by Marina Peres bears cutouts outlined with the image of vertebrae at the sides of the waist.

On the screen, a giant eyeball peers around as though astonished by what it sees. The electronica dance music continues as Ania Trublaska appears in a shiny gray dress with a steely industrial look. Egle Tvirbutaite goes by in a marvelous black leather coat over leather pants and a sheer top embroidered with black flowers. Jourdan Dunn, the last model to walk, sparkles from her shoulders to her toes with real amber crystals. She makes her turn and marches back toward the giant restless eye as the lights fade.

Unusually for a McQueen show, there are no grand theatrics. Even more unusual, the models are all smiling as they take their final turn. And then a huge fluffy animal appears and takes a bow. It's McQueen in a blue bunny suit. The show ends on an upbeat note, with smiles all around. The audience is smiling, too, particularly the buyers. In the showroom, there will be lots to buy, lots of wearable clothes. But some viewers feel a bit let down. Where is the darkness? Wher e are the McQueen fireworks? Or has all that been put aside in the names of commerce?

Opposite page: Egle Tvirbutaite wears a black leather jacket and trousers with a sheer top adorned with embroidery.

Above: Crystals, like the ones represented in this engineered print, have long been valued for their beauty—and more recently, for their many technological uses.

Right: The weight of Jourdan Dunn's crystal-covered showpiece bodysuit restricts its wear to the catwalk.

THE HORN OF PLENTY

Fall/Winter 2009–10

At first glance, the woman's image, complete with white wimple, looks like a painting by a Dutch Old Master. With more attention, the image proves to be a photograph—a photograph of a woman with a plastic shopping bag on her head. This is the invitation to Alexander McQueen's latest show. In the center of the square stage at the Palais Omnisports de Paris-Bercy hulks a huge pile of refuse: tires, old computer keyboards, burned-out televisions, an uncoiling hose, car parts, antlers, broken chairs. Cracked mirror tiles make up the surface of the catwalk, as if all this debris has crash-landed.

The trash onstage is not the only thing that's crashed. Financial markets worldwide have plummeted, and economic conditions are grim. So, what better time to look back and engage in some recycling? This collection references and subverts vintage Dior, Givenchy, and the entire haute couture tradition. McQueen also refers to earlier collections of his own, and props from his earlier shows adorn the trash heap.

The models wear grotesque makeup—huge painted-on lips—and towering shoes. Many of them walk with their hands on their hips and strike poses using stylized gestures that evoke vintage glamour. The Philip Treacy headgear, which includes umbrellas and soda cans, lends an extra dose of surrealism. The music starts—a roar—the lights come up, and the first model steps out onto the shiny cracked-glass catwalk.

Covered in hounds-tooth plaid, Alla Kostromichova makes the first run. Not only is her coat patterned, but also her boots, leggings, and sunglasses. The hounds-tooth references Christian Dior as does the shape of the outfit. With sloping shoulders, nipped-in waist, and full skirt, it's very "New Look," the style that Dior pioneered in 1947. Hanna Rundlof wears a stiff boxy jacket and straight skirt that seems a caricature of a Chanel suit. On her head, she wears a lampshade covered with red feathers. Next comes a hounds-tooth suit embellished with squiggles of white that are reminiscent of a Jackson Pollock painting. It's shown with the studded choker and wrist cuffs of fetish wear.

Amanda Laine wears yet another hounds-tooth plaid suit, shown with a metal choker that recalls the neck rings of the Padaung women of southeast Asia. McQueen has presented clothes with a choker like this before—in his fall/winter 1997–98 collection "It's a Jungle Out There." This look also refers to John Galliano, who included a similar choker with a "New Look" suit in his fall/winter 1997 collection for Christian Dior. Still more hounds-tooth goes by, including a fur coat. Hannelore Knuts in knitted hounds-tooth coat and pants, poses with particular grace. Removing her hands from her pockets, she flexes her wrists and turns one hand over, gesturing in the direction of her walk, a glamorous mime, a silent-film star from another era.

Left: Hannelore Knuts, all in hounds-tooth, is a vision of exaggerated glamour.

Opposite Page: As Alla Kostromichova walks, the fur on her hat, which resembles thick, glossy hair, bounces with her movements.

Tao Okamoto, in a billowing harlequin outfit and towering pumps with platform soles that each have two stacked pointed toes, walks with ease, one hand on her hip, the other arm swinging. She stops to pose, toying with the bow at her neck and peering at the audience coquettishly. Two more hounds-tooth ensembles go by, and then the looks are all black—coats in a fabric that looks like plastic trash bag, but is actually a silk blend, a strappy ruffled dress worn with a leather harness and impossibly high boots. Heidi Mount wears a black sweaterdress that seems to absorb the light around it. With knitted coils on her head and around her neck, she conjures Medusa, the angry mythological monster, whose image is said to fend off death. As the epitome of fatal attraction, Medusa has been used since the late 1970s as the logo of the Versace brand.

Two more sweaterdresses, a furry-looking black one with a signature corset belt and a hooded black and red striped number, go by. Then Liu Wen walks out in a strapless dress with a hemline that rises above the knee in front and falls into a long train in back. On the sound track, a steady drumbeat, what sounds like the baying of wolves—a possible reference to McQueen's "Supercalifragilisticexpialidocious" show (fall/winter 2002–03)—and an avian squawking. The pattern on two dresses was inspired by M. C. Escher, the master of tessellation, and depicts magpies, probably the most intelligent bird. Wearing the second version, Anastasija Kondratjeva walks demurely, her arms at her sides, hands hidden in the folds of her dress. Then she poses, throwing her head back and flashing a manic smile.

Opposite page: Liu Wen's umbrella hat is by Philip Treacy for Alexander McQueen.

Right: The knitted snakelike coils around Heidi Mount's head and neck recall Medusa.

To a syncopated drumbeat and more wolf howls, Raquel Zimmermann slinks along the catwalk. Her dress, a reference to Yves Saint Laurent's wrap dresses, glitters from head to toe with paillettes. She poses, hands on hips, leans forward, then back. Stepping off again, she casts a disdainful look behind her. The howling on the soundtrack intensifies, and Karlie Kloss in another tesselating magpie-print dress, this one floor length, comes out, followed by Vlada Roslyakova in a fitted strapless gown that flares out just above the knees and forms a rippling train in back. Small red and black feathers cover Roslyakova's dress from top to bottom and even embellish her shoes.

The print of Charlotte di Calypso's gown looks like a pile of red coral snakes. The mermaid silhouette is typical of McQueen evening wear. Di Calypso is rather hobbled by her dress and moves slowly. She poses, pressing her hands together, fingers pointing down, a lost sisterhood's warrior salute. At the back, her dress has an open hoodlike shape that recalls a Comme des Garçons design from the 1990s. Her silver chain-mail shirt and face mask are recycled from McQueen's "Eye" collection (spring/summer 2000).

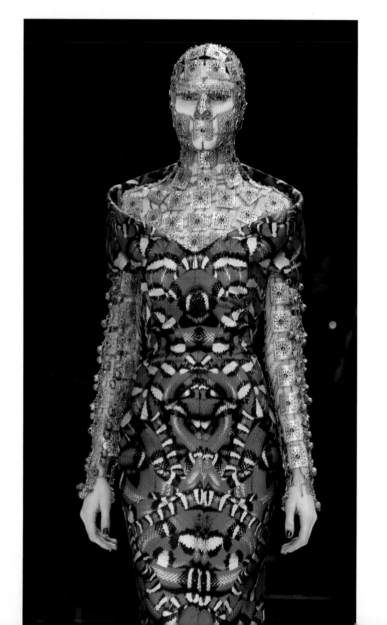

Left: Charlotte di Calypso's silver chain mail by Shaun Leane for Alexander McQueen appeared in an earlier show over a bikini bottom and heels.

Above: With different makeup and styling, Raquel Zimmermann would look quite glamorous, perhaps even red-carpet ready.

Opposite page: Karlie Kloss in a magpie print. In addition to being very smart, the magpie figures in a number of European superstitions.

"I think it's dangerous to play it safe because you will just get lost in the midst of cashmere twin sets. People don't want to see clothes. They want to see something that fuels the imagination."

—Alexander McQueen

Right: *Ever a stickler for details, McQueen has made sure that Polina's dark lipstick exactly matches the shade of polish on her fingernails.*

Opposite page: *Magdalena Frackowiak's dramatic black feathered dress ends the show with a flourish.*

In another gown that narrows at the knees, Polina advances along the catwalk in small careful steps. Her long cloak appears to be made of Bubble Wrap, but was milled for McQueen from silk and synthetic fibers. In another take on recycling, the garbage-bag material of the ruched dress was fabricated from nylon. Sigrid Agren's dress, inspired by Matthew Bourne's *Swan Lake*, is crafted from white duck feathers. Magdalena Frackowiak plays the black swan as she takes the last turn. In contrast to the dark feathers that cover her head and neck, her heart-shaped face glows white. As Frackowiak walks, the music fades, leaving a beeping sound, the sound of a heartbeat underneath. The heartbeat stops. And much like the end of "Pantheon Ad Lecum" (fall/winter 2004–05), the machine howls, a cry in the face of death.

Reaction to the show is mixed. Some critics are ecstatic, proclaiming that McQueen's provocation is just what fashion needs, a shaking up in hard recessionary times. Others are disturbed by the apparent misogyny of the grotesque makeup and dangerously high shoes. There is agreement, though, that McQueen knows how to create a spectacle, and his clothes, even if theatrical, even when parodies, are beautifully executed pieces of great imagination and technical perfection.

PLATO'S ATLANTIS

Spring/Summer 2010

With this event, Alexander McQueen opens up the exclusive world of the fashion show to the general public. In collaboration with award-winning photographer and web publisher Nick Knight, the show will be live-streamed to the Internet. Knight estimates that, in the month following the presentation, as many as 40 million people worldwide will watch the video of the show—constituting a huge expansion of audience. Another draw: chart-topping singer/songwriter Lady Gaga has just announced via Twitter that the recording of her latest song will debut during McQueen's show.

Foreseeing a time when the polar ice caps have melted and the seas have risen, McQueen predicts a future in which humans, with the aid of bioengineering, reverse evolution and return to the sea from which all life came. "Plato's Atlantis," the title of the show, refers to the legendary island described by the classical Greek philosopher as having sunk beneath the sea. McQueen explains that this show is based on fantasy, myth, and legend. He sees Atlantis as a place "where people find sanctuary in bad times."

On the catwalk at the Palais Omnisports de Paris-Bercy, two robotic cameras greet the audience. The cameras move the length of the white catwalk on tracks, their snake-like necks following the models' movements. Images from the cameras are projected live on a screen at the back of the stage, which is designed to look like a white-tiled laboratory, suggesting that each model is a biological experiment in evolution. The models' makeup—whited-out eyebrows, built-up cheekbones, and "gills" at the temples—emphasizes the hybrid theme.

On the screen, Raquel Zimmermann lies in the sand, writing as snakes slither over her naked body. She gathers the snakes in her fists, clutching them to her, and they morph into a symmetrical pattern. The robotic cameras pan the room, projecting the audience onto the giant screen. Then the screen goes white, and the first model appears, a silhouette against the brightness.

Magdelena Frackowiak, dressed in a digitally engineered snake print, marches the length of the catwalk in snakeskin "Armadillo" boots so phenomenally high that she seems to be walking on her toes. With their futuristic styling and twelve-inch height, the boots are a sensation. More minidresses go by, each with a unique engineered print.

A hissing breath, like that of a scuba diver drawing air from a tank, fills the room. Zimmermann is back on the screen, floating on her back, her face and breasts just barely breaking the surface of the sea. Many in the audience find the scene anxiety provoking. Presumably for McQueen, a trained scuba diver who has said that he is at his happiest when diving, the hissing of air and underwater images are intriguing, perhaps even comforting.

On the catwalk, the dresses change to the swirling blues of aquatic life. As the transition to the undersea world becomes complete, the shape of the models' faces begins to change as they turn into alien life forms—a hybrid of human and sea creature.

Opposite page, left: Yellow enamel paillettes emphasize the narrow waist of Magdalena Frackowiak's short dress.

Opposite page, right: To create Tanya Dziahileva's gray frock coat hybrid, McQueen draped a jersey shift on a mannequin, cut up a tailored coat, then fused the two together. On her feet, Dziahileva wears a pair of iridescent "Alien" shoes.

Right: Alice Gibb looks like undersea royalty in a short gold dress covered with beads and pailettes and bejeweled "Armadillo" boots.

"I don't think it makes sense to play safe in these times. The world needs fantasy, not reality. We have enough reality today."

—Alexander McQueen

Left: Michelle Westgeest's sheer organza top gains structure, sparkle, and drama from metallic threads.

Opposite page: Iridescent enamel paillettes completely cover Polina Kasina's jellyfish outfit and "Armadillo" boots.

On the soundtrack: drumming. The images on the screen swirl, like cells dividing, reproducing. Short jellyfish-print dresses match the colorful moving background. The beautifully puffed sleeves of Uliana Tikhova's mini create a sort of ruff around her shoulders, the pleats and folds like gills. Tikhova is followed by four models wearing sheer iridescent organza in amorphous shapes. The four look as if they've actually become jellyfish. On the screen, a creature—is it human, a sea monster, or a hybrid of both?—slowly waves its arms as if dancing in the surf.

A luminous Polina Kasina takes the stage. Glowing in the low light, she appears to be some bioluminescent undersea being, the queen of the deep. Applause breaks out and Lady Gaga's new song "Bad Romance" starts up as Kasina finishes her turn, walking toward her own projected image. The image fades and the lights come up. As the models all take a final turn, the cameras point their snake-like snouts at the spectators, projecting them on to the screen. McQueen comes out, in his usual jeans, to cheers. He waves and quickly ducks away.

McQueen has long embraced technology and the Internet. In 2004, he provided a pattern for free downloading on SHOWstudio.com. With "Plato's Atlantis," however, he breaks new ground. Suzy Menkes writing in the *International Herald Tribune* describes this show as "the most dramatic revolution in twenty-first-century fashion."

POSTHUMOUS COLLECTION

Fall/Winter 2010–11

Alexander McQueen's latest collection, unofficially called "Angels and Demons," is scheduled to be presented in Paris at the Conciergerie—one of his favorite venues—on March 9, 2010. Everyone is working feverishly to prepare for the show. McQueen's mother, Joyce, died on February 2, and McQueen wrote about it on Twitter the next day, ending with "RIP mum," followed by a long line of x's. The youngest of six children, McQueen was close to his mother. She attended his presentations and was a great supporter of his work. The day before her funeral, McQueen is found in his London flat, dead by his own hand.

New York Fashion Week has just begun. The shocking news spreads quickly. Some editors rush out of shows in progress. As they did in London, people leave flowers and notes in the designer's memory on the sidewalk outside the Alexander McQueen New York flagship store—just down the street from one of the presentation venues. The showing of his McQ by Alexander McQueen line, which is scheduled for New York, is canceled. His Paris presentation is also canceled.

A week after McQueen's death, representatives of the Gucci Group announce that the firm will continue to finance the Alexander McQueen label. In addition, small groups of editors will be invited to see McQueen's fall collection in Paris on March 9 and 10. Sixteen ensembles, which were 80 percent finished at the time of his death, are chosen. Editors sit on boxes, two or three grouped together, at the Hôtel de Clermont-Tonnerre, an ornate eighteenth-century mansion.

McQueen's work on this collection was inspired by Old Masters and Byzantine art. The work of Grinling Gibbons, a sculptor and woodcarver whose work adorns St. Paul's Cathedral and Hampton Court Palace, and the paintings and altar pieces of Hieronymus Bosch, Sandro Botticelli, Jean Fouquet, Hugo van der Goes, Jean Hey, Stefan Lochner, and Hans Memling also figure in this collection. True to the tradition of handcrafting and the great artisans that were so important to him, McQueen cut each pattern himself.

The proceedings are somber, much like a wake. One by one, the models appear in the mirrored salon. They move slowly, with a stately grace. The soundtrack consists of classical music, what McQueen himself listened to in the weeks before his death—"Dido's Lament," from Henry Purcell's seventeenth-century opera, *Dido and Aeneas*, sung by the German soprano Simone Kermes.

In this collection, McQueen joined images from the past with current technology to create extraordinary work. Images from religious paintings were electronically scanned and woven using digital technology. A pattern of angels appears on one dress and at the back, the image of a pair of wings. Embroideries echo the religious theme. And there are prints of birds as well as underskirts and entire garments of feathers. Polina Kasina, who served as McQueen's fit model for many years, comes out in the final ensemble—a spectacular jacket of gold feathers with a high stand-up collar worn over an embroidered tulle skirt (page 210).

The dresses, cape-like coats, and one pantsuit of this final collection memorialize their maker and his extraordinary craftsmanship. His talent, showmanship, and passion— a bright light in the increasingly corporate and gray world of fashion— are, and will continue to be, missed.

Opposite page, left: Posing in front of a gilded mirror, Karlie Kloss is regal, a futuristic queen.

Opposite page, right:
Alla Kostromichova's dress is crafted in a silk jacquard bearing images from Hieronymus Bosch paintings. The bodice is embroidered with gold sequins.

Right: Here, Alla Kostromichova wears a coat fit for a cardinal. When she walks, the sequins on her dress rustle.

Flowers left as a tribute to Alexander McQueen line the sidewalk outside the designer's store in New York City.

EPILOGUE

As dean of the School of Fashion at Parsons, The New School for Design, I am notified of anything that affects the students' well-being. Thus, I got a text message on February 11, 2010, to tell me that Lee Alexander McQueen had died and students were crying in the corridors.

I don't know how many of our students had chosen fashion because of Lee's work, but I know most of them wanted to either work for him or be him. It is hard to overestimate the effect he has had on young designers—and, no doubt, will have on the generations of designers to come. In fashion, we are naturally wary of the term *genius*, but if it can't be applied to Lee then to whom?

Many times I heard from friends in the industry that after seeing the 2011 exhibition "Alexander McQueen: Savage Beauty" at The Metropolitan Museum of Art they needed to sit somewhere quiet and reflect. I know I did. You expect that from an exhibition of Rodin's or Picasso's work, but a fashion designer's? Attended by more than 650,000 people, "Savage Beauty" was the biggest Costume Institute show in the Met's history.

Lee McQueen was ferociously creative. And he had a laser-guided vision of what he wanted to do. He was a designer, an artisan, and an inspiration to so many creative people around him. Accomplished designers would shake their heads in wonder at what he could drive them to do when they worked with him. He was utterly uncompromising in his vision. Whether it was a tiny detail, a grand ensemble, or an entire show, he applied the same degree of attention, the same dedication to perfection, the same vision. And so we needed a moment to rest and reflect after each of his shows.

And now, sadly, we have time to reflect on his body of work and see what a genius he was.

Simon Collins
Dean, School of Fashion
Parsons The New School For Design

PHOTO CREDITS